THE ARMIES OF THE ANT

THE AMERICAN MUSEUM OF NATURAL HISTORY'S

THE NEW EXPLORERS

GENERAL EDITOR:

ALFRED MEYER

THE ARMIES OF THE ANT

BASED ON THE EXPERIENCES OF

DR. CHARLES L. HOGUE

CREATED BY ALAN LANDSBURG PRODUCTIONS, INC.

WORLD PUBLISHING
TIMES MIRROR
NEW YORK

ACKNOWLEDGMENTS

I was never really alone at the Rincón station. Life was made bearable during difficult times, and work a pleasure always by the presence of my comrades Julian P. Donahue and Andrew E. Williams. Life itself would have been impossible without the logistical support of the Organization for Tropical Studies, arranged by Jorge Campabadal, a man who understands the laws of supply and demand.

My thanks are extended to Leslie R. Holdridge and Joseph A. Tosi, Tropical Science Center, for use of their facilities, and to A. Wright, Osa Productos Forestales, for his many kindnesses and for those of his staff at Rincón.

Finally, for the opportunity to live again in the rain forest, my adventurous soul expresses its gratitude to Alan Landsburg Productions, especially Alan himself, Larry Savadove, and Howard Lipstone.

This book is
dedicated
to the courageous and dedicated
explorers and scholars
who have led us behind the Green Curtain

Contents

Foreword

The exuberance of the first night of my visit with Charles Hogue at the Organization of Tropical Studies' research station on the Osa Peninsula in southeastern Costa Rica took, from my point of view, a heavy toll. It was not only the combined influence of heat and the very palpable psychological pressure of the looming vegetation that led to such an unforgettable numbness the following morning. It was also the intemperate consumption of that imperialist staple of tropical environments, that purportedly antimalarial potion, English gin and quinine water.

To be sure, I was at first rather perplexed to find that Hogue was not, at this phase of his adventure, as completely alone as I had been led to expect. Whereas I had conjured up the classical vision of a solitary researcher slogging his way through the matted biology of the rain forest, I found instead a whole cast of characters clustered at that remote but well-stocked and sunny station. In addition to a gardener, a cook, an ornithologist, and Hogue himself, a team of West German entomologists had lately taken up temporary residence. It was, incidentally, the head of this team—a man whose name I involuntarily suppress—who unwittingly contributed to my vast discomfort, as I will explain shortly.

"The New Explorers"—of which this volume is a by-product—is fundamentally a series which puts a seasoned biologist rather than a camera crew behind a motion picture camera. The reasoning behind this intelligent departure from routine practices is simple. Adequately filming even a few of the complexities of life in a natural habitat is ordinarily a long and arduous business, principally because the life cycles of flora and fauna blithely adhere to their own, nonhuman, rhythms. Consequently, when the film process attempts to focus more intensely on an ecologic situation, it is often victimized intellectually and aesthetically by economically dictated filming schedules, by the uncooperativeness of nature, and by the usual inexperience of professional film-makers with biological phenomena.

The strategy of "The New Explorers" is to solve the first two problems by insisting that its "hero" be on location long enough to be able to come away with more than superficial footage. In terms of the third problem, the organizers of the series have found that it is far easier to teach a biologist to use a motion picture camera than it is to teach a cameraman biology. Moreover, cameramen, being for the most part very civilized human beings, do not readily take to prolonged periods in the wild. On the other hand, certain biologists, although presumably equally civilized, display on occasion a zestful willingness to isolate themselves for months at a time in order to study the behavior of such far-flung creatures as wasps, baboons, aardvarks, or desert rodents. And since their scientific passions often know few bounds, they tend—in pursuit of evolutionary exotica and behavioral niceties—to trot off to those points on the globe calculated to produce absolute maximum human discomfort. Behind this seeming masochism, of course, lies an ordinary and generally applicable piece of logic: where people don't go much, there plants and animals are apt to be playing out their indigenous life patterns, exempt from human influences.

Such an intrepid and adventure-loving biologist is Charles Hogue, although he sometimes—unaccountably in my opinion—forgets himself and claims that he loves civilization more than he does the flight of the glass-winged butterfly through the ferny corridors of the rain forest. And such an inhospitable place is the Osa Peninsula where sits the research station, a rational and scientific speck on a wild and pulsing sea of tropical forest. Ultimately, all "The New Explorers" series does is bring the three—biologist, camera, and in this case, rain forest—together and await the offspring.

On second thought, there was nothing unduly inappropriate in finding Hogue and the station inundated with visitors. The gardener and the cook were more or less permanent fixtures who lived nearby. The ornithologist, working on a grant from the Institute for Vertebrate Zoology in California, had come to collect eggs and nests. And each of the three members of the German team had long nurtured the idea of an extended insect-collecting trip in the tropics, and had realized their ambitions by coming to this insect-rich part of Costa Rica. To tell the truth, under the circumstances I was probably the most intrusive member of that select and short-lived little group, having come down neither to garden, cook, nor practice science, but to acquaint myself with Hogue and the rain forest and to see firsthand a genuine army-ant colony.

The carnivorous army ants are unquestionably one of the world's most spectacular life forms and have received considerable exposure in popular literature. Their raiding behavior is legion, and the periodicity of their nomadic and statary phases, as well as their high level of social organization, has also long been the subjects of intensive and often distinguished scientific investigation, particularly that of the late T. C. Schneirla of the American Museum. Although Hogue, a trained taxonomist, was not to be involved in a structured and formal investigation of the ants, they very quickly became the most compelling subject he found. And if there was an ulterior delight underlying my editorial visit, it centered on the prospect of being able to stand within a foot of a raiding party. Happily, I did so, the gesture, however, proving absolutely unprovocative to the ants.

But the details of the life of the army ant must properly be left to Hogue's own narrative. Let me return to that first balmy night. The atmosphere at the station after dinner quickly became convivial, perhaps even boisterously so. Polite, of course—but nevertheless reserved and studious—the German team grew noticeably uncomfortable as Hogue and I waxed loquacious on matters great and small. I had, in regulating my personal behavior that night, counted it in my favor that of everyone in the room, Hogue had been the first at the station, and so had staked it out territorially. Although the others were by common consent equally entitled to the facilities of the station, they clearly deferred to Hogue and had therefore to suffer, in addition to the most uncomfortable beds and the least amount of working space, the tedium of listening to our rambling conversation. This phenomenon of personal space and territoriality at research stations, by the way, has not to my knowledge been fully documented. Nowhere have I encountered such rigid rules of interpersonal behavior, and, consequently, such a high level of interpersonal tension, than at research stations or on scientific expeditions. The station in Costa Rica was no exception.

The leader of the German team, a smallish, bearded

scientist in his early thirties, eventually busied himself
—rather pointedly I thought—with mounting the insect
specimens he had collected that day. His wife, a stun-
ning and decidedly un-Germanic creature, puttered about
delicately with her Leica, while the third member of the
team, decked rather incongruously for the tropics in
lederhosen, escaped outside to pick luna moths off the
large white collecting sheet that had been spread beneath an insect-attracting ultraviolet light next to the
station.

Hogue and I continued on insatiably, and loudly
exhausted every available subject: the role of science in
society, the history of rain-forest exploration, the wick-
edness of man, and finally the problems Hogue was having living in the tropics. Through the conversational
haze, I began to perceive how different a human being
Hogue was from the first "New Explorer," T. J. Walker,
a difference so great it approached the difference between the tropical rain forest and an Alaskan lake.
Walker was a shaggy and brooding figure who con-
fronted his six months at Lake Eva in southwest Alaska
with the settled determination of a religious recluse.
Introspective and obsessive, he trudged through the
swampy trails of the cold northern wilderness with an
almost grieving consciousness, murmuring incantations
to the fish and the birds. Hogue, on the other hand,
young and insouciant, seemed at first unfettered by that
northern involution of spirit. Effervescent, bright, and
as pragmatic as the manager of an A & P, he viewed his
role in the "New Explorer" scheme as a temporary job:
film the rain forest and its creatures, particularly the
army ants, and record personal and professional observations on a tape recorder every day. Period. Then
go back to being curator of insects at the Los Angeles
County Museum of Natural History.

"I want to get the filming done and the recording
sessions finished and then I want to get the hell out," he
offered, looking absently over to the plucky German

scientist who, with infinite grace, was mounting an astonishingly large and fierce-looking beetle.

Hogue squeezed a blighted lime over his glass.

"I'm not one to rhapsodize much, nor do I like to go very long without my comforts, chief of which, I might add, is my wife," clucked Charley, frowning absurdly.

Pragmatic Charley, managing an A & P, shrugging off the rain forest, shrugging off his own elegant sensitivity to the biology of the tropics. Sheer empty bravura, I concluded, secure in knowing that the transcripts I had seen of his tape-recording sessions totally belied this gratuitous disclaimer. For, sitting alone on a stump outside the station with his tape recorder, nowhere to go beyond the perimeter of his own green clearing, perhaps even with nothing much to think about *except* the goddamned forest, Hogue spills it. The eddies of wind in the forest, the mysteries of the upper canopy, the rush of the rain, the clacking of the toucans, the filtered light. Those wisps of northern Anglo-Saxon reflection coming in like gusts from Alaska.

The Germans reassembled and retired en masse punctually at nine o'clock, barely concealing, as they moved up the narrow staircase leading to the sleeping quarters on the second floor, their collective disapproval of the general ribaldry taking place below.

Then Hogue was seized by a new inspiration and applied himself to the shortwave radio to see if he could raise his father in Sacramento. I, meanwhile, attempted unsuccessfully to feed an apple to a caged pair of six-inch-long dynestes beetles, while Andy, the ornithologist, wielding a silver pipette, blew the yolks out of a half-dozen tinamou eggs he had collected that morning. Adding to the din, and to that generated by the crickets and katydids out in the night, was a low grumbling and an unmistakable sigh or two from upstairs.

A short while later, I became aware that there resided in my own mind a certain wariness about the inhabitants of the rain forest. Despite a conscious skepticism of the commonly exaggerated terrors of the "jungle," I found myself reviewing with Hogue and Andy the dangers lurking about me. Who has not read of the terrible and swift venoms discharged by New World snakes, or of the stealth of vampire bats who apply local anesthesia before imbibing warm vertebrate blood so they may go unnoticed, or of the bizarre reactions engendered by the bites of strange spiders, or of the weird and improbable paths tropical parasites take through living human tissue in order to reproduce?

"Calmness is everything," pronounced Hogue darkly.

"Not to worry," said Andy.

I went to bed vaguely reassured and fell asleep trying to make order out of the cacophony of the night, and dreamed of jaguars.

The next morning I awoke dazed and exhausted. Slipping on a robe, I painfully made my way down the stairs and headed to the wooden shower stall. I turned a corner and had just begun reaching for the door of the shower stall when my heart froze in utter terror. All the primitive fears I had dismissed the night before now rushed instantaneously through my brain. Whatever it was I had stumbled over, it was huge and alive. I yelped and clawed desperately in the air as I went down. The insanity of the moment trebled when I landed on top of it.

If my relationship with the head of the German team had been chilly it was now positively frigid, for there he lay, sprawled next to me. One cannot, it appears, trust an entomologist. Turn your head and he immediately starts groping about some crucial corner looking for an insect. He had evidently spotted some six-legged treasure crawling innocently out from the stall and had scrunched down on all fours to apprehend it. It was at that moment that I had so blindly sallied forth. We did not speak to one another thereafter.

* * *

Strictly speaking, you have before you neither literature nor science but a bastard product, the edited transcripts of Hogue's recording sessions. Accordingly, Hogue must not be held responsible in the conventional sense and should be regarded as a supplier of raw data rather than an author. Yet, for all the obvious vulnerabilities inherent in this electronic resurrection of the oral tradition, there emerges in these pages not only a picture of the biology of the rain forest but, equally important, a distilled and haunting sense of how the beauty of the forest affected a gifted and unusual man.

ALFRED MEYER
Editor, *Natural History* magazine

THE ARMIES OF THE ANT

1. An island reversed

The upper extreme of the Golfo Dulce. Rincón is located on the other side of the upper point of land. The gulf is very deep and navigable by large ships all the way to Rincón.

I awoke to the sound of birds and katydids and the droning of cicadas. My view from the window where I sleep is a solid wall of green foliage broken only by the vertical, light-colored trunks of various trees and the occasional deep brown branches of palm trees. Vines climb up the trunks of many of these trees, so my first sight each morning is the forest. It imposes itself upon me from the very instant I wake up, and stays with me all day until I go to bed at night.

This feeling of greenness is beginning to come over me. I felt it before when I've come to the tropics, especially during the rainy season when the vegetation is even greener than it is now. Your eyes become addicted to green as the predominant color. Suddenly, I can't remember the grays and browns of the temperate regions, especially of the southwestern United States,

1

southern California, where I live. No, the green becomes ingrained. It seeps into your skin, and saturates the retinas of your eyes. It is almost as if your whole visual system and brain were impregnated with the forest chlorophyll itself, and you begin to photosynthesize the light, and inside your head it takes over your thinking.

Let me describe a scene that is before me at the present time. There stands a large pool of water, some fifty feet long, about twenty feet wide, about three feet deep. I've watched this pool of water grow and recede with the rains. Now it contains half of what it did when I first arrived here, and the stream is running about half a foot below what it was. The pool is exposed to the full sunlight. Now it looks like something that might be observed on the planet Venus. Cords and wisps of intensely green algae are proliferating, lying in a slimy tangle. The algae is gradually taking over the pond, and the water in the pond is assuming the same green that prevails in the leaves of the trees. It seems almost as if the water has dissolved the green from the air, put there by a gaseous aerial absorption, and is concentrating this green and turning it into the stringy cords of algae. It is another emphasis of the movement of green from one state of matter to another, the solid of the green leaves of the trees to the gaseous state of dissolution in the air, and from the air to the liquid state in the water of this pond, and gradually back into a solid state in the form of algae. It is another kind of cycle: it's a cycle of green, a cycle of the metamorphosis of chlorophyll. Perhaps it exists only poetically, but it does seem to be going on here. Or could it be that the rain that falls on the leaves absorbs the green and transfers it down the trunks of the trees and off the tips of the leaves and into the water of this pond, where it is concentrated in the swirling masses of algae again? What sort of metamorphosis can be imagined with the green that is so prevalent in everything that exists here?

I am even turning a little green myself. I have mentioned how it affects the eyes. It absolutely affects what I wear. The leather of my belt and my machete case, left unattended for two or three days, sprout a lovely greenish growth of fungus and I have to brush it off. My shoes turn this color if left unwashed, my briefcase, nicely polished with wear when I came here, has been sitting unattended. I looked at it the other day, and, on every exposed piece of leather inside and out, I found a carpet of greenish mold an eighth of an inch deep. It's impossible to escape from it. When I was walking back through the water, having been caught in the rain, I was wearing a pair of low safari shoes which are a kind of olive-green color. When I took my shoes off, my feet were completely soaked, and I found that they had become stained green. To look at them was like looking at the feet of an imaginary green child from another world. My feet are still stained this green color. It's entirely appropriate to this place, and I actually feel that when I do leave here and return to Los Angeles, for several days the water in the bathtub after my bath will run green down the drain like some biological ink.

Approach to the landing strip in front of the station. Dodging the hill in the foreground is a good test of a pilot's ability.

OVERLEAF:
Stringy green threads and gobs of algae give this sunny pool in the quebrada a semblance of some extraterrestrial landscape.

I am outside of the research station now and looking around for a good spot to sit down, a spot where it is quiet. Even though this is a very peaceful place, it is difficult to find a spot where there's little noise because of the abundant animal life, particularly birds. At this time of the evening (it's about five o'clock now), the parrots are coming in in great numbers. They find themselves a good tree and they come in and mass, making as much noise as they possibly can.

I just spotted my first toucan. I don't know what species it is, but it's mostly a black bird with yellow markings and, like all toucans, has an enormous beak. They are amusing to watch when they fly because of their long protruding bills. The bird almost looks as if it were pushing a banana along in front of it. I've heard people refer to them as flying bananas, but this is an affront; they are beautiful birds, their colors are brilliant, and they sit in the dead trees around the edge of the station here in the evening and make their calls.

I can pick up one new sound after another: katydids, cicadas, crickets, frogs, some with the most bizarre sounds I've ever heard. As I listen, I hear the sound of someone vomiting, the sound of a Coke bottle being hit with a sharp metal instrument, and the sounds simulating the chirping and cheeping of birds. They all blend together and make one sound, a singular sound, which is reproducible nowhere else on the Earth, except in the recesses of the rain forest.

I'm in a little clearing here. I can look around me 360 degrees, and I see a wall of green punctuated only by the upright white trunks of many trees. It's common for trees here to have light-colored trunks. But when you look at a tree trunk here you don't always see the trunk itself. Dozens of different forms of lichens grow upon the bark of the trees and give them color and texture strange to trees. And as I look around me, I see this undulating and pervasive wall of green, and a few tree trunks, and I feel as if I'm on a reverse island, an island

that's not surrounded by water that I can look down upon, but rather an island that's depressed, and I have to look up, up to the sea of green around me.

This afternoon I made a trip down to the nearest settlement, Rincón, which is some miles from here. Rincón means *corner* in English and was chosen by its founders because of its location in the upper end, or corner, of the Golfo Dulce. It was an arduous journey but one which gave me great satisfaction. It was a simple thing to do. I went down there just to introduce myself to the people, and made the journey back in the sun of the afternoon; but I did some things, some things happened to me, which made me realize, made me remember once again, that I'm an animal. I don't mean this in a degrading sense, but I mean that it made me remember that I'm made of flesh and blood and that I have body systems and functions like those of other animals. We tend to forget these things when we live in the city. When we

A species of *Steirodon,* a giant katydid of over three and one-half inches in length.

OVERLEAF:
Ghost of a dinosaur? No, a male elephant beetle (*Megasoma elephas*) plodding laboriously along a tree limb.

7

The function of the head horn of the elephant beetle is still not known in spite of the large number of them collected by entomologists.

get in an automobile and go to work, sit behind a desk, and go through the motions of putting together a work day, we constantly de-emphasize our human nature. I think we actually forget we are humans, and by forgetting that we forget that we are also animals.

For the first time in many months I felt the taste of salty sweat in my mouth and on the tip of my tongue, as it dripped down off my nose and upper lip. I stopped for a moment to rest in the shade and I looked skyward to see a vulture circling overhead. Suddenly, I felt the burn of salt water in my eyes as the perspiration ran down from my forehead into my eyes. These are joyous things. It sounds strange, but they're joyous things because they do make you remember your connections, your relationship with the natural world—not only looking at it, experiencing it with the eyes and ears but actually working with it, letting the air run over your

10

body, water run through your body and out your pores, feeling the hot sun beat down on your forehead. These are all sensations that gave me some real joy this afternoon, though I wasn't even in the forest. My muscles have gotten flabby, but I made the trip all right and I'm very happy that it came off so well.

In my few minutes of peace and quiet, usually after I awake in the morning, before I get out of bed, and before I get to sleep at night, I mull over in my mind and think about this forest and what it is. I'm going to be talking from time to time about my ideas and the ideas of others as to what the rain forest is, what its soul is, what its function is, and what of it might be useful to man. As a biologist, I'm mainly interested in ecological aspects, and I have read textbooks and many papers about the ecology of the rain forest, but I still don't see it all. I say *all* because it is difficult not to think of the forest as a single unit, as a single organism rather than as a group of associated organisms. As I look around me, I don't see a group of trees inhabited by living animals and insects; rather, I see one, one thing, one organism with its elements partly hidden, partly exposed. Much of this is due to the density of growth, the closeness of the trees, and the intertwining of the branches, so there actually is an interconnection, a physical touching of the different elements of the rain forest. This is not found in many other types of plant associations, at least not with the ones with which I'm more familiar—the desert formations in the Southwest, where the trees and other plants are wildly scattered. Because of the scarcity of water they have spaced out over the land, and as you walk among them you see them as units separated from one another. But here, just the opposite occurs. You see the trees as a part of one another, they are touching, they are in intercourse, and form a real network which can be thought of as a whole. This wholeness has been appreciated by scientists for a long time, and I think it has contributed to the fact that the rain forest has served as

the primary model of an integrated ecosystem. Rain forests are out of the way, they're off the beaten track, they're in the tropics, it's difficult to reach them. Nevertheless, the relatively few early visitors to the rain forest, those who were educated as biologists one hundred years ago when ecology was just being born, were struck not only with its great beauty but by its continuity and by its singular aspect. When life is so exuberant, so abundant, and so many things are going on, biological interrelationships become gloriously conspicuous.

I must mention that I saw today another one of these creatures by which one cannot avoid being startled. This is a tiny larva of the lacewing fly, which has the curious habit of picking up bits and pieces of debris, little chips of wood, little flecks of dirt, pieces of leaves. Somehow it affixes these to its back. When this little animal walks along, it carries its pile of rain forest. Julian named it a true "mobile mound of detritus," a little movable midden mound. (I should mention Julian here parenthetically. He's a temporary resident moth collector who night-hawks all the wonderful creatures of the dark and his ultraviolet light lured endless new discoveries.) The insect puts this habit to use when it stops, however, for it normally rests on bark which is encrusted with lichenous growths. When it holds perfectly still among the growths, it blends in perfectly with its background. So its burden is not a burden but a suit of camouflage which will protect it.

As I look into the gray sky, I'm experiencing what little bit of dusk there is here in the tropics, in the mid-latitudes. Those of us who are used to the twilight which comes with the dawn and the dusk of every day in the temperate regions rarely get used to the phenomenon of the tropical sun coming up and going down with a thud. Right on schedule every morning the sun pops up over the horizon without announcing itself, and after a neat twelve hours drops abruptly across the opposite horizon and it's night. Twelve hours of night and twelve hours of

OPPOSITE:
Different species of the genus *Polybia* construct paper nests which are all highly characteristic in shape.

OVERLEAF:
The Hercules beetle (*Dynastes hercules*). The incredible fact about this ponderous beetle is that it can fly. INSET: This specimen forced its way out of a wire birdcage.

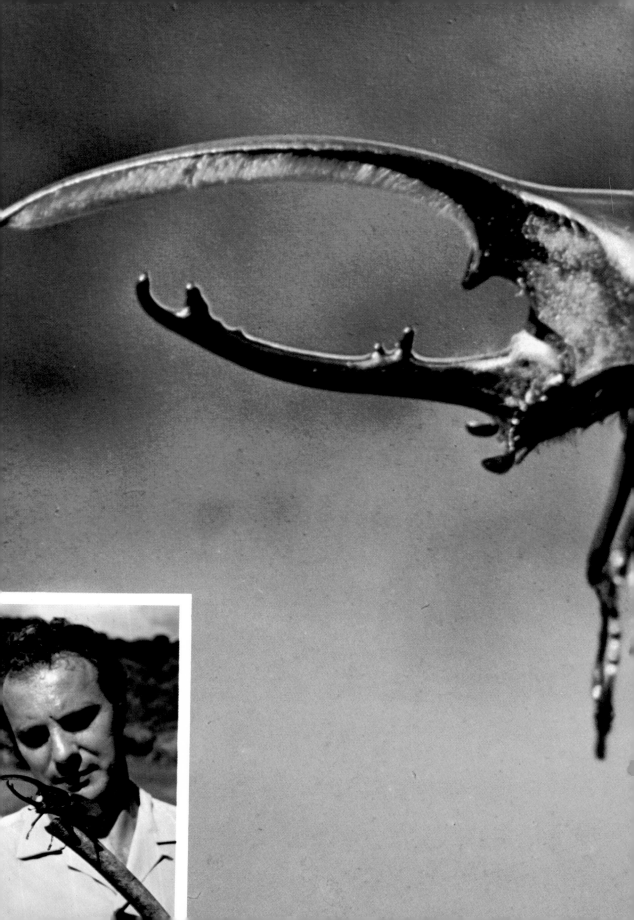

It pays to be cautious when approaching a nest of *Synoeca surinama.* These wasps have an aggressive disposition and a painful sting.

Synoeca surinama at work on an addition to their paper nest. The internal combs and outside sheath are built simultaneously. The compartment will soon be closed except for an opening at the top.

day, twelve hours of night and twelve hours of day, and thus it goes on throughout the year with little variation.

It's a little later now, and the sounds around me are increasing in intensity and can be described (if I had to do it in a single phrase) as an intense buzzing, the same kind of a sound I remember at home on the morning of a rainy day when the high tension wires, which were wet from the fog and the dew and the recently fallen rain, would buzz and hum. But here, of course, the sounds are not coming from a metal wire but from live organisms, hundreds of different kinds, hundreds of animal musicians, most of which are insects, primarily cicadas and katydids. The sound is much the same, and the feeling you derive from it is much the same. It is a feeling that the air around you is alive, your environment is alive, the very air you take into your lungs is alive. You *feel* the life around you. In the temperate areas, so much of our lives seems to be played out in a dead environment. We have asphalt, we have concrete, we have bricks and mortar and plaster around us, and we have sound emanating from machines, which are built with dead material, steel, iron, copper. But here the things around you are alive, you breathe in life, all your senses are perceiving life. The experience is absolutely luminous.

2. The ambience of the night

The katydid leaves her nymphal skin, which becomes a pale apparition while the newly metamorphosed adult hardens and turns green like the leaves around it.

Almost every night I have crystal-clear sky and I can see the stars. Because of the latitude here I cannot see Polaris, the North Star. I could if I were on the ocean, because I am 9 degrees north latitude and the star should appear at 9 degrees, above the horizon. However, there are hills to the north of the station, and Polaris hides just over the crest of this range of hills. I can see the big dipper swinging around, arching around the sky, around Polaris, but I cannot see the star itself. . . . Oh my God— behind me, fantastic, one of those beetles, those fluorescent beetles. There's another one, absolutely incredible —it's like a fireworks display. There's a beetle here of the genus *Pyrophorus* which has two headlights on the front of the thorax and another light organ on the underside of the abdomen . . . there's one next to me. And there's another out over the stream. They're not like fire-flies that flash on and off. They glow, they glow in a steady stream of light which flows through the forest. I just saw four of them, and what a sight: the light is so bright that it actually lights up the leaves beside the beetle as it flies. It's a streak of light, it's the fourth of July; it's really bright, it's a greenish fluorescent light, an uncanny light which I've never seen before. I wonder if my flashlight is attracting them. I'm going to take my flashlight and I'm going to flash it around in the forest and see if I can't possibly stimulate some of these beetles to flash. Oh, there's one, a bright spot of light sitting on a plant only twenty feet from me. It's grad-ually fading out. . . . it has come on again, and now it's fading out again. The beetle is obviously resting on the plant, throwing its light and then letting it fade out. There's another off to my left and another and another. The stars have fallen into the forest among the leaves of the trees.

I'm flashing my light. As I flash it around through the understory of the forest, I seem to stimulate the beetles into glowing. When they go through the air, it's sheer pyrotechnics. Now I'm going to flash my light up into the canopy. There don't seem to be any up there. I'm going to sweep it around the understory again. Ah, as soon as my light comes near a beetle, on comes his light, just as if it were a reflector alongside of a road as you see it when you're driving in a car in the dark of the night. Every time I turn around there's some other un-believable thing to see. There are two of them now where there was one before. It's like coming out and looking at the horizon on a clear night, and seeing the stars grad-ually coming into view as the sun goes down and the sky darkens. There seems to be just the right quantity of light coming from my flashlight to ignite these *Pyrophorus*. . . . Oh, my God. There's one that was bright, bright orange, like a falling star or a burning match or a sparkler thrown through the air. One could easily use these beetles to live by, to read by. They're like meteorites falling through the forest. This is a sight I can hardly believe; I shine my light on the tree and it's like looking at a Christmas tree, it lights up, absolutely incredible. I say my name, Charley Hogue, Charley Hogue. The night is real, it is real, and I don't know what to do I am so bedazzled.

Several days have passed, and I have not forgotten the ambience of that improbable night. But let sweet reason prevail. Why do the big click beetles, the ones with the two headlights in front, produce this strange light? Are they imitating the behavior of the fireflies, the lampyrids? Normally, among fireflies the females emit a glow, and the males respond to it with a signal of their own. The females then respond with another glow, and the males gradually zero in on the females so that they can mate with them. But all is not always romance: Now, there happens to be a certain firefly (*Photuris*) which is predacious on a closely related firefly (*Photinus*). They produce a sham signal to attract the males. But instead of mating with them they attack them and feed upon them, clearly an aggressive use of a mimicking signal of light. It is like a submarine in wartime flashing its light to an unwitting freighter. Knowing the code that is used by the freighter, the submarine gives it a signal— one conveying a sense of security, albeit false—to enter the harbor. When the freighter does, the submarine attacks with torpedoes and blows it up. It's essentially the same situation.

A phenomenon occurs here which can be appreciated only when you go into the forest on a moonless, pitch-dark night and walk down the trail without a light. If you do so, you will see something very beautiful and unusual. This is the luminescence given off by dead, rotting tree trunks and branches. Apparently, there are bacteria and fungi which are responsible in part for the

OVERLEAF:
Behind the station, at the edge of the clearing, light has stimulated an overabundance of viny growth which fits the layman's concept of the "jungle" more closely than the ordered layers of the forest proper.

decay process of dead wood, and these produce a luminescence, a photochemical reaction which gives off light. Thus you can observe this soft, greenish, cool, ghostlike light emanating from logs and branches in the forest, and in the pitch of night, it's almost like a soft, ghostly picture painted in the darkness. You would get the same feeling by having a large, luminous clock face stare at you unexpectedly in the night.

This is the eighth of April, and you're going to think I'm crazy. I was sitting out in the front of the station here in my chair enjoying the sunset and evening when I saw an unidentified flying object. I swear you're going to think I'm out of my mind. I've lost a little bit of my mind, I admit at this point, but I saw it, I yelled and I screamed and I called Andy, an itinerant ornithologist

The light filters down to the forest floor through the leaves of *Cryosophila,* the only palm in Costa Rica with fan-shaped leaves.

visiting the station. He came out and he saw it, too. It was a light, a starlike light, moving from about southeast to the north, and it was moving at a rate of speed far in excess of the capabilities of any aircraft. It was obviously in the atmosphere. It wasn't a star or a meteorite. It moved continuously in a straight line from over my shoulder, where I first saw it, to the point where it reached the horizon in the space of about thirty or forty-five seconds. It was a fairly bright light, with an intensity approximately equal to a medium star. Then it went down beyond the horizon.

There's no explaining it. It was not an airplane, it was not a rocket ship, it was not a satellite. I've seen satellites, and I know how they move. They move in a steady pace very slowly across the azimuth. It was not one of those. It was something I can't explain, and it is the first time in my life I've ever seen anything like that. I'm a believer now, I am a believer that there is something going on which we don't understand. I have to join the group of people who are not believed and who are thought of as crazy, but there it was. Absolutely two of us saw it. It was there. What was it? I just asked my temporary cook about it. She is a Costa Rican woman, and said that she has seen the same thing here. She has seen them many times. I don't know what it is, but the sky is so clear that there may be something about the tropic latitudes that has attracted these things. But what are they? I saw it, Andy saw it, and the cook saw it. It was a light moving across the sky, and it was moving too fast for an airplane or a satellite, and it couldn't be a star. So what was it? I ask you.

3. A splendid pillar

Linguita Creek. This crystal stream was tapped for the station's water supply. It flows year round from springs.

Yesterday, the station was invaded by army ants. I came back to the station after being out on a little hike to find one whole corner of the building simply crawling with thousands of worker army ants. They come into the cabin to search for insects on their normal scavenging raids, and you might easily conclude that they are a good form of house cleaning. I have my own house cleaning service, insect eradication service, thanks to the ants themselves—without the danger of insecticides, moreover. They stayed around for only a while, about an hour, cleared out, and marched on down through the forest. Presumably, they are bivouacked nearby, in an area which I have not yet found.

Few of the trees here are known to me now. I've

studied a little bit of tropical botany, but this is an overwhelming problem. There are between two and three hundred species of trees in the area around the station. I'm used to living in the northern latitudes where there are fewer than a third the number of species. Even at home I have to continue to go back to reference books to remember the names of the different kinds. Here I'm lost. It's as though I'm in a crowd of people whose names I don't know. I see the same person pass by me from time to time, and maybe if someone tells me his name I may be able to remember it. It's the same way with the trees here, only trickier. I have been told the names of a few, like the *Cecropia*, with its palmlike leaves, and the balsa tree, with its large, broad, ovate leaves. But except when I see these old friends I can't recognize them. Even professional botanists who are making concerted efforts to study and classify the trees in the rain forest have the same difficulty. This is largely due to the fact that the classification of plants is based upon floral character-istics and the anatomy of the flower. The flowers on these trees in the rain forest often bloom some hundred to one hundred and fifty feet off the ground, and it's no small problem getting a specimen of one of these flowers. Some botanists in the Old World trained monkeys to climb the trees for the sole purpose of collecting specimens of branches and flowers, and bringing them down so that they could then examine and classify the trees. Even where a sample of a leaf or flower is within reach, you can never be certain that you have a piece of the tree itself. This is a taxonomic hazard caused by the great amount of epiphytic plant growth here. The word *epiphyte* literally means "plant upon," and it refers to plants that don't maintain contact with the ground but rather find root upon the branches and trunks of other plants. They actually grow upon other plants. They're not parasitic—not all of them, at least—but they use the other plant as a foundation just in the way that most normal plants use the earth. They obtain their nutrients from the air and water, and in fact produce a kind of soil themselves way up off the ground in the canopy of the forest. So you might walk up to a tree and take a piece of leaf off of it, examine it, classify it, and decide that it is characteristic of the tree. But, often enough, such a process is sheer delusion, for go two feet farther up, pick off another leaf, and you're likely to find a leaf entirely different. Epiphytes truly confuse the picture.

I'm looking up at the sky now and I see gray, because it's approaching night and a few clouds are wafting in. This is the middle of the dry season, yet we're still seeing some of the transitional features of the rain forest leading from the wet season to the dry, particularly the coming into bloom of numerous trees. A few clouds are passing over. I haven't seen rain for three days. Even in the dry season, however, I can expect to have a little bit of rain from time to time. I'm looking forward to this because even here in an area of intense rainfall, one feels a sense of dryness on looking up at the trees and seeing some of the epiphytes actually drooping and drying up. It does seem strange that in a tropical rain forest plants can dry up and become crisp and brown, and loose their turgidity. But I have seen this in the last two or three days.

The station here at Rincón has two stories: upstairs I sleep, downstairs I have my kitchen, my main workroom, my bath area. I have a nice shower, water comes down to me from one of the mountains surrounding the clearing. Pure water. It has been tested and found to be surgically pure, with practically zero bacterial content. This is very reassuring, for often in the tropics the water is contaminated with disease-producing organisms. I have plenty of water even in the dry season. The stream which is tapped for my water supply runs with full force, obviously being supplied by some sort of an underground system. I have the basic accouterments of

Threatening skies. Rainfall at Rincón exceeds 200 inches a year, and rain falls almost daily even in the dry season.

civilization in the normal home, such as a stove, a refrigerator, and electricity, at least during that part of the night that I run the generator. I use this electricity primarily to recharge the batteries for my cameras. It also gives me light to read by and light to learn a little bit more from the small amount of literature that I have brought along, of the very small amount that exists, describing the life of the rain forest.

The *Cecropia* tree is a common weed species that
springs up in clearings. It is
a good indicator of disturbance of the forest by man.

4. An unexpected visitor

The smooth, pale tan bark of *Terminalia lucida* peels off the trunk in long strips. Botanists suggest that this may be an adaptation for sloughing epiphytes.

Someone recently made an attempt to paint the station white, but, in moist areas such as this, buildings tend to deteriorate very quickly from mold, and from the attacks of termites. Frame structures, such as our station, can't be expected to last very long.

We have screens on all the windows. This is essential here because there are biting flies, many of which are active at night and some of which carry disease. Malaria occurs all along the coasts of Central America, but it's very spotty, localized in certain areas. Here at our station at Rincón we are relatively free of it. There's another little fly here, however, which carries a similar menace. This is the moth fly, belonging to the genus *Phlebotomus*, a name by which it is usually referred to. Here in Costa Rica, it is called a *papalomoyo*. These are tiny little flies with hairy wings, so tiny that they can fly through a normal screen. They bite readily, and those which happen to be infected with the organism of leishmaniasis can transmit them to you. If conditions are just right, the organisms multiply in your skin and produce an ulcerish growth which spreads and can be rather disfiguring and very uncomfortable. The disease is called muco-cutaneous leishmaniasis, and it may occur here around the station. The flies are most numerous in the deep forest. They rest in shaded places, protected places, such as in the buttresses of large trees, underneath fallen logs, rot holes in trees, and so on. People who spend much time in the forest run a good risk of being bitten by these flies. During the days of intensive exploitation of chicle in the rain forest regions of Brazil and Central America, workers who harvested the gum naturally spend a lot of time in the rain forest. They were bitten by these flies and developed this quite common disease, and these workers, because they harvested the sap of the gum tree, were called *chicleros*, and the disease which they frequently contracted was called *oreja de chicleros*. The flies, for some peculiar reason, very often bite the earlobes or the skin around the ear. In the old days it apparently was common to see a "gumpicker" with his ears either grossly deformed or lacking completely because of this disease.

However, in general, I am quite pleased by the absence of biting, bothersome insects here. I still haven't seen many mosquitoes, for example, but I do have some interesting bites. They're on my ankles, and I don't know how in the world they got there. Although I've been wearing high top boots, I have a series of oozing, reddish sores which I suspect have been caused by bites or stings of ants which have gotten down into my boots. I'm going to have to take special care to treat these with antibiotic salves so that they don't become infected.

I have to mention also that I've acquired a very intimate new friend. For the last three or four days I've had a little itchy bump on the top of my left foot just between the base of my fourth and fifth toes. At first, I assumed this to be nothing but an especially pesky mosquito bite and did not pay too much attention to it. After taking a shower I got outside and noticed that in addition to itching, this little lesion was also giving me sharp, shooting pains. It still didn't dawn on me what might be happening. The following day when I put my foot out in the light and took a close look at it with a hand lens, I could see some movement in the little circular opening in the skin. I had been brought to the realization that I now had my first parasite. Although I studied medical entomology and parasitology in college and spent a fair amount of time in the tropics, it was not until that moment that I could make the proud announcement that I was wearing my first flesh parasite.

The parasite turned out to be the larva, or maggot, of the human botfly. This fly is quite abundant here and has an interesting life history. It is large and heavy-bodied and resembles a bumblebee. An agile and fast flying insect, it has nevertheless in the course of evolution found it advantageous not to lay its eggs directly on its host. Possibly its resemblance to a bumblebee frightens the host and makes it difficult for the fly to come in and lay its eggs. Instead, it has acquired the curious habit of laying its eggs on another insect, usually a fly or a mosquito. Flies and mosquitoes attain ready access to vertebrates, landing on them, visiting them all the time. The vertebrate hosts, including man, pay little attention. Apparently I've become a victim of a mosquito biting me on the foot when I was out at night in front of the station barefoot. The mosquito transmitted the young larva to my skin. The eggs are carried by the mosquitoes and inside the eggs the larvae are already well developed. Upon contacting warm vertebrate skin they hatch and pop open immediately and the young larvae drop to the skin and burrow in.

I'm not sure what to do about this little fellow. He

OVERLEAF:
The station building. The forest was literally at my back door. Sleeping quarters are upstairs; kitchen, bath, and work area downstairs.

has caused some consternation and it is a little difficult to walk. I've had quite a bit of bleeding from it too. But I think I'll leave him there for a couple of days to see what happens. I don't think it's a good thing to ignore it too long, however. I've read accounts of entomologists who have allowed these maggots to go to maturity in their own bodies and it's quite a distressing tale to read. They are extremely painful when they grow large. The bodies of these maggots are covered with tiny little recurved spines and when the larva rotates in its little feeding cell it causes a great deal of pain to its wearer. So I think I'll try to get rid of it by taping down a piece of bacon over the little pore. The reason there is a little pore opening in the skin is that it provides access to air for the larva. The larva has two tiny breathing pores at the posterior end of its body, like little nostrils. It backs up to the opening, projects these out into the air, and thus obtains its oxygen. That is why I have the little pustule or pimplelike opening on the top of my foot now. Fairly common in Costa Rica, they are known locally by Spanish name, *tórsalo*. While they do occur in humans and are called the human botfly, they are actually found more commonly in cattle and other animals.

The last two or three days I have been talking to various people in Costa Rica via the ham radio network. Half a dozen or more Americans live down here in various places and have radio sets. I have talked to them from time to time and one of the subjects that has come up for quite a bit of discussion are the *tórsalos*. It seems that there is much that is unknown about the medical aspects of this fly, as well as of its life history. It is very much more common than I expect and several of the people that I have talked to have had experience with it. One of the men who lives in Quepos, probably a hundred miles from here, has a young son who just recently had an infection. The man removed the maggots from his son's leg and had been describing to me the symptoms.

One of the most significant facts, one I was unaware of, was that it is very possible, indeed common, to have more than one maggot in the same wound. Apparently even three maggots have been observed in a single wound. This is an indication to me that there is no migration of the young maggot after it enters the skin. What probably happens is that upon contact of the carrier fly with the eggs and the skin of the human, two or three eggs hatch simultaneously, the larvae burrowing into the same immediate area. As the larvae's feeding areas gradually become confluent, a single large wound develops containing two or three maggots. Thus it is possible to remove one maggot and still have problems. Apparently this is what happened to the boy. His father removed one maggot, which was fairly good-sized, probably about two-thirds mature. The boy showed some improvement but then quickly relapsed into a fever with inflammation around the affected limb, extreme pain, and copious wound-festering. Obviously, no improvement. The father checked the wound carefully and determined that another larva was inside. By using what is known as the bacon treatment, he got the maggot to protrude most of its body and he was able to catch hold of it with his fingers and pull it out. The boy showed immediate relief from the pain and swelling.

I am happy to report that I too took leave of my intimate friend, the maggot, by taking the advice of one of the locals who also recommended the bacon treatment. Last night on retiring I taped a fatty piece of bacon, about half an inch square, over the opening in my foot where the maggot was. I taped it down very tightly, covering it with a Band-Aid to exclude as much air as possible, and I left it on all night. The next morning, after breakfast, I peeled off the tape and the bacon and found the maggot wound was quite heavily festered. By exerting gentle pressure on either side of the wound I was able to cause quite a bit of pus to exude. It seemed that the area was loosened up by the drawing action of

Hogue at the worktable in the station. The transceiver in the background kept me in touch with the outside world.

the bacon so I gave it a good hard squeeze and, bang, out came the maggot, complete. I cleaned the wound with sterile tissue and carefully picked off the maggot, which seemed to be dead by then. I preserved him in a little container of alcohol and finished cleaning up the wound by putting some antibiotic salve on it and bandaging it. I felt greatly relieved to have this critter out of me. It was beginning to bother me a bit. There are precious few insects in this world I don't like or can't handle, and one of them is the maggot. I examined the specimen with a hand lens and, sure enough, it was an instar, or second stage, larva of a *Dermatobia homanis*,

40

which is the human botfly, a member of the family
Cuterebridae, which includes many other botflies, which
prey on rabbits, rodents, and other animals.

This brings up the subject of the dangers in the
New World rain forest. The most insidious dangers arise
not from large animals that might attack me in the
forest in the daytime, or might bother me in my nightly
wanderings; it really comes from the small insects which
I mentioned before, from such as *Anopheles* mosquitoes,
which carry malaria. There are others, of course, and
many biting and stinging forms don't inflict a great deal
of harm in themselves, but if you don't take care of a

sting or a bite, it can become infected through scratching, or a severe sting can cause a great deal of swelling and pain. So the insects are by no means the most benign life form in the rain forest. They can cause a great deal of trouble. Of course, so can snakes. Speaking of snakes, we do have a nice repertoire of poisonous species here: the fer-de-lance, the bushmaster, rattlers, and the coral snake, to name only a few of the obvious ones. Yes, I suppose these can be classified as dangers.

There's a parrot flying right over my head now, and I enjoy watching the way it flies. It seems that just the tips of the wings vibrate up and down, while the base of the wings remain relatively stable. It reminds me of the way in which the wings of a large jet liner bounce up and down when they're going through rough weather. The parrot is an interesting bird to watch in flight because its head and neck portions are as long as its tail portions, so that the bird forms a kind of X-shaped figure in the sky, whereas most birds have a longer tail and look more streamlined as they fly. It is close to dusk, so the swifts are on the wing too. They fly around catching insects that are active at this time of the day, and they give the air a vibration by the rapid flipping movement of their wings. The swifts will soon be joined by insectivorous bats, and as the sun goes all the way down the swifts will cease to fly (being crepuscular birds), and the bats, which are nocturnal, will then come down. It is all so nicely timed.

Oddly enough, one of the pleasures of the station is the lawn. The grass is kept cut fairly short by local laborers who come in from time to time with their machetes, there being no such thing as a lawn mower around here. I also have a unique feature to my lawn. I don't have many flowers growing on it, although many grow around it, off on the edges. But I have just as much color as any flower garden, for, from about nine o'clock in the morning till the sun starts to get low in the early afternoon, a tremendous number of different kinds of butterflies float through the grass and light on the lawn in the front of my house. I'm sure if I sat down and tried to count the number of different species that it would count in the tens. They like to congregate around one corner of the cabin, near the front door. I'm not sure exactly why. They may pick up some fruit odors from the kitchen. But they're all kinds and they're all colors, and my lawn is decked with shimmering jewels.

It's very obvious to a person walking through the forest that the wind passes through the branches and among the leaves in very curious pathways. I frequently notice out of the corner of my eye a leaf or a branch of a tree waving wildly or bobbing to and fro for no apparent reason. There doesn't seem to be any wind blowing, any breeze, but in actuality there are tiny pathways, wind currents that form through the branches of the trees. These currents are caught by leaves and branches, and they react to them by wild movement which startles the imagination. Yesterday, I observed the tip of a fan palm which was bobbing back and forth, back and forth, swaying in the breeze in the midst of the rest of the forest, which was perfectly still. It was almost as if this tree were alive in itself, and moving like an animal trying to wave to me, trying to give me some sort of signal. After a little while, the breeze that was causing this phenomenon died out, and the tree quieted.

After walking a short distance, I found a log of a tree that had been cut fairly recently, probably less than two or three months ago. The wood had split rather severely where the tree had been severed from its base, and in the time since the tree was cut, a great deal of sap has oozed out of the fallen, wilted trunk. This exudate has started to ferment, decay, and break down organically, and is attracting some very curious insects. I carefully turned over some leaves which had floated down onto the trunk and had become stuck in the exudate, and underneath them there were a number of small beetles. I remember one in particular, one belonging to

the family Histeridae. These are medium-sized black beetles which are often attracted to animal carrion. This fellow was pretty well buried in the exudate. He extricated himself from the sticky mass and slowly and laboriously crawled across the trunk and down the side. Apparently, the odors emanating from these decomposing, fermenting exudates are very similar to those emanating from chemical substances associated with the decomposition process of animal tissue. The odors are similar enough so that they attract similar insect forms, and one finds basically the same kinds of beetles and flies at both rotting stumps and on freshly killed animals. The odor similarity is apparent even to the human nose, I hasten to add.

A very large (one and one-half inches long) member of the click beetle family (*Chalcolepidius porcatus*).

I suddenly found a very large beetle, a member of the family Elateridae. These beetles are called click

44

beetles, because when they find themselves on their backs for some accidental reason they can right themselves by snapping their bodies. A tongue-and-groove mechanism on the underside of the body connects the front part of the thorax with the rest of the thorax. The body can thus be made to snap sharply at about a 10-degree angle as the beetle is lying on its back, and this snapping action propels the beetle into the air. Chances are he'll come down and land on his feet. If not, he'll snap two or three times more and eventually right himself. The sound that these gymnasts make is a snappy, clicking sound, hence the common name. While I watched the click beetle I noticed a beautiful spider wasp searching, crawling around in the litter near the base of a log, even crawling over my boot from time to time. She looked like she was hunting in search of something, so I watched her for a while. Eventually, she came out from beneath the little pile of leaves struggling with something, and on closer inspection it turned out that she was holding onto a large spider, a species with an extremely large, round abdomen, light gray in color. She struggled with the spider a little bit and then started to crawl up my leg. I reacted, naturally, by kicking her off, feeling that she might decide to sting me. In so doing I disturbed her, and she dropped the spider into the leaf litter again. I lost sight of it. She flew around for a few seconds, landed on the ground again and then began searching once again, crawling over and through the leaf litter. Sure enough, after two or three minutes she found her spider again. I disturbed her again, and again she lost her spider. She flew around a bit, came back, discovered her prey a third time, and proceeded to haul it off underneath her body. Apparently, the weight of the spider was too great for her to pick up and fly with so she was carrying it, slung under her body, with a spare pair of legs, crawling with the other four. She bore quite a bit of weight, and her actions were rather cumbersome, but she managed to cover a distance of ten or fifteen yards. She reached the

Flies and wasps are often found locked in a death grip to a leaf. The fruiting bodies of parasitic fungi reveal the cause of this fly's demise.

A bracket fungus (probably *Hydnum* sp.), one of the many molds that attacks dead wood and aids in the decay process, reducing cellulose to simpler compounds.

base of a large tree and began crawling up, as if she knew where she was going. She was going to a very definite place. She probably had a nest high in the tree somewhere, possibly one made of mud, as many spider wasps have, and she was taking her prey to provision the nest for the developing brood which was undoubtedly in the nest. This wasp was steely blue in color, very beautiful in the bright sunlight, and quite large, about an inch and a half long.

A short distance from my log I found a short piece of rotten log, a piece which had been broken and had lain on the forest floor for some time—I would estimate, several years. It was supporting a luxuriant forest of light-colored fungi. These are probably bracket fungi, and indicate that the decomposition process of the log had proceeded to a considerable degree. I noticed a small lizard, the American chameleon, belonging to the genus *Anolis*. These lizards are not the true chameleons, which are

African animals, but they're the ones that are sold in pet shops and they do have the ability to change the color of their skin from brown to green. At any rate, I spotted one of these little fellows jumping from leaf to leaf. He finally came out from behind the trunk of a tree, and he seemed to have something in his mouth. I looked more closely and found that it was a spider. But there was also an insect in the vicinity of his mouth, flying and flitting about in toward his head. It turned out to be my spider wasp, and I'm quite sure I can figure out what happened. The lizard had simply stolen the spider from the wasp, and the wasp was fighting to get his prey back. The lizard won, and proceeded to munch on its prey for some time. I was very surprised during the middle of this process to see the lizard display his dewlap. The dewlap is a large, extendable membrane beneath the chin of certain lizards, which they can extend at will. The dewlap is always brightly colored, and in the case of this little *Anolis* was an orange color with a brown speckling. The display of color has at least one function that I know of related to sexual display. It apparently brings the female lizard into a proper state of excitement or acceptance preparatory to mating. While watching the lizard, I sat absolutely still, and I was amazed how many other insects and birds buzzed around me.

I noticed a stingless bee, a species with an orange abdomen. These bees were particularly interested in the thick resinous material which was oozing out of one side of the stump, and they seemed to be gathering it and chewing it and picking it up with their mandibles and sticking it to their legs and carrying it off. I believe they use this material as an adhesive substance, and mix it with wax, which they secrete from their own bodies, to form their nests. It is a construction material, a natural mortar that they use in their nests.

Then, out of the corner of my eye, I saw something flutter, turned, and I couldn't believe what I saw. I saw four spots of color. Two of yellow, two of steely blue-

black moving up and down, a blur. It took me a minute to realize that this was one of the giant damselflies that occur here in the rain forest. They are absolutely beautiful. The tips of the wings are colored, and the rest of the wings are translucent. The body is very frail and fine, so that most of the animal is invisible or appears only as a wisp of gossamer light, and the eye sees only the tips of the wings moving up and down. They fly like ghosts through the forest.

A brightly colored cockroach crawled across a leaf. An *Ameiva* lizard rustled in the grass beside me. He came out from the shade and was posing very handsomely in the sun. All of a sudden behind me there was the loud crashing of a branch high up in one of the trees. As the branch fell to the ground, there was a great deal of commotion and noise. I was nearly scared out of my wits because I couldn't determine exactly where the branch was going to fall. From the sound I knew it was

This minute fungus displays amber droplets of fluid at the tips of fruiting hyphae. The spores presumably are nurtured and suspended in this medium to be spread by wind when the droplets dry.

Though considered a lower form of plant life, this fungus displays a complexity of structure and reproductive physiology that is no less fascinating than that of a flowering plant.

a big one, and I was afraid I was going to be hit by it. I have been in the rain forest before and experienced this same phenomenon. Apparently, branches on the trees get heavily laden with epiphytes, and then they rot and lose their strength. Gradually, their weight tolerance limit is reached and they come crashing down with a stupendous noise. Such an event can be dangerous if you

happen to be in the wrong place at the right time. Since that time I have heard whole trees fall with an even more awful crash.

The whole story of what happens to a fallen or a dead tree in the forest intrigues me. If there were no decomposing organisms on the earth, we would soon be up to our necks in cellulose material. The vegetation that grows around us—branches, twigs, leaves, trunks, roots —is primarily cellulose, made up of chemicals derived from the air and soil, oxygen, water, and nitrogen. If this were allowed by nature to accumulate deeper and deeper, there would be no replacement of these nutrient materials to the soil. Thus, where there might be luxuriant growth there would soon follow sterility. Many forms of insect life play an important part in the decomposition of this cellulose material, and I think I'm going to try to follow this dead log of mine and this tree stump while I'm here and see if I can't determine the stages of decomposition and the various spectra of insects associated with each of these stages. The stump is fairly fresh and most of the insects that are working it now are not directly involved in the decomposition process. Some are not true decomposers but are utilizing the exudates of the tree as a food or as building material, as in the case of the stingless bee. However, inside the log, invisible to me now, I am sure that various wood-boring beetles, termites, and even ants are performing a first stage, major physical breakdown of the trunk of the tree. There is on the trunk very little surface area in relation to its mass, so that the actions of much smaller organisms such as the bacteria and fungi are not able to carry out their decomposing function very effectively. It is the larger insects which riddle the wood, burrow through it, and break it down, grind it up and turn it into sawdust and fine particles. Such carpentry increases the surface area of the cellulose, and encourages the decomposition process work in its early stages. Then the bacteria and fungi can work in earnest.

I don't know whether it's because this is the dry season or whether events are just falling into place at this time, but I have become fascinated with the nutrient cycle, the return of organic nutrients which have been manufactured in the leaves and eaten by the consumer organisms back to the soil via leaf drop, the droppings of animals and through the death, decay, and decomposition of animals. In the grass outside of the station a couple of days ago a snake was killed by one of the men cutting grass with his machete. It was a fairly good-sized boa, about six feet long. He left it there, and before very long it was attacked by turkey vultures, which took the greater portion of the meat off the bone. Then it was attacked by various insects, including wasps, flies, and other small meat-eating insects. In the space of two days, the snake had been reduced almost entirely to skeleton. The dry weather has slowed down the normal decomposition by bacteria and fungi, so there still remains dried skin and dried muscle tissue on the skeleton. But it is being removed bit by bit, particularly by wasps. I suspect that the flesh will be completely consumed in a day or two.

I also collected a bat a couple of nights ago with a net and hung it up in a cage. I promptly forgot about it and discovered today that it had died. It was beginning to deteriorate and beginning to take on the odor of decay. I put the bat out on the ground to see what the progressive stages are in decomposition. The decay odor was quite strong, even though the bat was very small. About an hour later I noticed a couple of turkey vultures circling above. I know from ornithologists that this particular vulture locates carrion both through its olfactory and visual senses—often at astonishingly great distances but usually only in clearings. There is another species of vulture which lives above the canopy, circling about, but can find carrion deep in the forest interior by picking up the odors of dead animals relying primarily upon its ability to smell. This is the king vulture (*Sarcoramphus papa*). It may use olfaction almost entirely when dipping into the forest. Vision, due to the dense growth, would not function well and following odor molecule streams on air currents *would* be the more logical method.

I see daily the manner in which material is circulated in the nutrient cycle within the forest ecosystem. These are processes that many people might not notice,

A bracket fungus with an
unusual stalk. These organisms are hard and woody,
unlike the majority of other
fungi.

Delicate molds are constantly luring your eyes downward. Though small, their importance to the life of the large trees is vital. Nutrients in the thin soil accumulate only through the decay processes of lower organisms.

An unidentified mold creeps over and into the bark of a dead tree trunk. This form may have fruiting bodies totally unlike the lacy fingers typifying it at this stage.

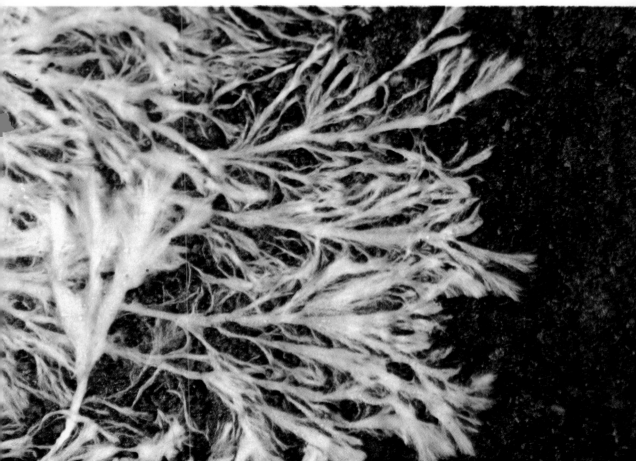

but which are fundamental in bringing back to the soil the minerals and other chemical substances that have been removed from it by the growth of the vegetation during the rainy portion of the year. Simple things like bird droppings, which are conspicuous on many leaves; they are of various colors and take various forms as they strike the leaves. This is material that has been processed by the birds through the fruit that they have eaten from the tops of trees, or from insects they have eaten, which in turn have eaten leaves and flowers of the trees. Another way in which the nutrients reach the soil again involves death of higher animals. It's interesting to note the various ways that death comes to animals here in the rain forest. On my way up the waterfall trail I stepped over a log and noticed the remains of a sloth. The animal may have been killed by man or by some predatory animal. Its skeleton and hair remained on the trail as a reminder of the fact that death comes to even the larger and better-protected animals of the rain forest. The sloth is a well-protected animal because its very slow movements, combined with its color, which mimics the lichenous and the fernlike and mosslike growths on the branches of trees, camouflage it well. The sloth is thus preyed upon by very few predators. At any rate, there were the remains of an animal relatively high up on the food chain returning just as certainly as a leaf or a dead insect back to primal elements.

A short way farther on I came across a caterpillar resting on a twig and completely immobile. On closer inspection, I noticed that the back of the caterpillar was completely covered by tiny little cocoons projecting out from the body. These cocoons, I knew from my reading, are those of a parasitic wasp which lays its eggs in the body of the healthy caterpillar. The larvae hatch from these eggs and burrow through the body of the caterpillar, slowly consuming its tissues—that is, all of its tissues with the exception of the muscles and digestive tract and other essential organs which keep the caterpillar alive and functioning so that the parasites will not kill the host. The larvae feed upon the contents of the caterpillar in this manner and gradually consume it from within. When they mature, they emerge from the caterpillar by burrowing out through the body wall, and then they spin these cocoons. Some caterpillars survive this final stage and actually go on eating and may even develop into a pupa. The example I found today, however, was a caterpillar which was totally paralyzed and completely motionless upon the branch. Whether it was dead or not was a matter of definition. Death comes to the creatures of the forest in many ways, and often so directly and violently that one can easily understand how natural selection works. It works on an accelerated pace in the rain forest where life activities proceed almost constantly throughout the year.

I'm standing here in the forest along my upper stream trail, and I think, just as an experiment, that I'm going to try to give you a blow-by-blow account of a tree.

I've walked up to a very handsome tree, and I'm going to describe it and what is around it and take a hold of it as I would a person, and see what the impressions are on me. I'm standing back now, about fifteen feet from the base. I must say it's a mighty tree. It goes almost out of sight up through the canopy of the forest. I can barely see the upper branches. But, coming out of the ground and spreading around the trunk in a circle with a diameter of about fifteen to twenty feet is the great buttressed base of this tree. The buttresses expand out radially in all directions but in a very irregular fashion. They are twisted, turned, and bear subdivisions which disappear into the ground.

The apparent function of these structures is support. I'm told by books, however, that this may or may not be the case. It would seem that here in the rain forest where the soil is shallow, a tree of such great height and bulk would need additional basal support to keep from toppling on windy days, and the buttresses would seem

OVERLEAF:
Like the arms of tiny vegetable hydras, the hyphae of this small fungus (one-quarter of an inch across) seem to be reaching out for more moist wood upon which to feed.

57

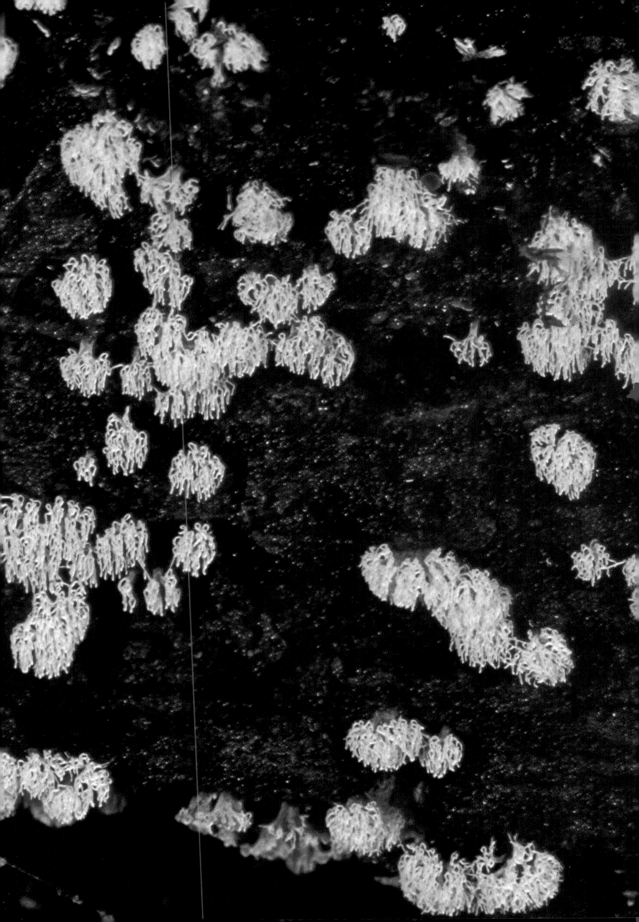

to perform this function. But, on the other hand, I can look around and see other trees as big but without buttresses, so this is still one of these unanswered questions. Now each of these buttresses is a great flanged plate. I'm walking over to the tree now and I want to point out that the wood is only about three inches thick through each of the buttresses. So, whereas they are weak in one plane, they provide a great deal of strength along the other plane because their breadths reach up to six feet. The buttresses taper. I'm letting my eyes run up the tree now, and I can see the breadth of the tree narrowing as the buttresses taper inward, and my eyes are now looking up at a height of about twelve feet. At this point, signs of the buttresses are almost gone.

The tree is quite densely clothed with epiphytes, and their variety is truly spectacular. There are great philodendronlike forms, leaves a foot or more wide and a foot and a half to two feet long. Others have thin, fine, stringlike stems twining up the outside portions of the buttresses, winding around themselves as well as the tree. There are two vines winding around themselves and yet a third vine winding itself around them forming a natural cable going up the side of the tree. Some of them continue on the main trunk, and others seem to be derived not from this tree but from other trees, and are interconnecting this trunk with others. These vines are called lianas, and they are the guy wires of the forest. They are probably responsible, much more than the buttresses, for supporting trees during winds by tying together the trunks in a great entangled mass of ropes and cables.

The trunk of my tree is made of very hard wood. The trees of the rain forest are all considered hardwoods —there are no conifers this far south—and some of these are among the hardest in the world. Certain woods here are so dense that a piece will not float in water but sink like a stone. Others are hard and almost metallic, so that a machete blade when struck against them rings as if struck against another piece of metal. About fifty to sixty

A tree festooned with epiphytes, mostly bromeliads and lianas, sending long, slender aerial roots to the ground.

Crooked lianas bridge the
space between trees and
help to support them in
windstorms.

The growing tip of a down-
ward-reaching aerial root.
When firmly implanted in
the ground, the shaft shrinks
and becomes as taut as a
violin string.

Fluted buttressing, a common type of trunk structure found in many tropical trees. The radiating flanges may help support the tree in the thin soil.

feet skyward the trunk passes through a layer of leaves coming from surrounding trees. By shifting my position, I can see through the lower tier of the forest and catch a glimpse of the upper canopy. It would take binoculars to make out any details because the apex of the tree is probably higher than one hundred and twenty feet. At that point, the crown of the tree spreads out to a number of bifurcating branches and forms an umbrella.

Certain types of epiphytes find a special niche of their own in the crotch or the bowl of a branch, and can grow to great luxuriance. This is where you find orchids most often, as well as certain types of epiphytic ferns and bromeliads. The bromeliad is a plant of the pineapple family which grows on the branches of trees. It is a true epiphyte. The leaves are elongated, usually spined

on the edges, and they spread out from a basal cup. The leaves are trough-shaped, so that they catch water; the water runs into the base of the epiphyte, collects there, and forms little pools. These little tanks of water, incidentally, support special populations of insects and other animals.

So my tree has bromeliads and orchids. It is also decorated with great, long, hanging, aerial roots coming from the crown of the tree. I pick one, and it is about a quarter of an inch in diameter and resembles a piece of smooth rope. Looking skyward along it, I can see it running absolutely and perfectly straight through the air, paralleling the trunk and disappearing into the canopy of the forest. If I pull on it, I find that it is resilient and rubbery and quite strong. I'm sure that I could hang on it, possibly without breaking it.

Finally, the tree has very thin bark, and, in many places, particularly between the buttresses, the bark is loose and peeling off. Also, much of the surface of the bark is covered by lichens and mosses. They give the tree a mottled appearance and hide the true color of the tree, which is a pale khaki or tan.

Would that I could give you the name of this tree, but I'm lost. However, knowing its name wouldn't add anything to its character, beauty, color, strength, massiveness, height, and sheer magnificence. It is an unbelievable edifice, a splendid pillar.

5. The orchid potion

The wind roared and roared. It is the first time I have heard the sound of the tropical rain forest bear any resemblance to that in the forests of the temperate regions. The wind whistled as it blew through the branches of the trees, and I could close my eyes and almost imagine that I was in a pine forest, except for the smell. With all this wind, the amount of leaf drop from the trees increased. And the wind disperses seeds and the fruit from the trees as the branches whip madly about. In watching the leaves falling from the trees and fluttering to earth—so like autumn—the similarity to the flight of numerous butterflies struck me. Yes, it might not be too farfetched to see in the drifting flight of such as heliconiids and sulphurs the twirling and wafting pattern of falling leaves. Insect predators ignore falling leaves.

Flowers of an unidentified species of *Sobralia*. It is a pity that these regal blossoms last only a day.

Rain often rides on the wind. Last night I heard the sound of rain coming. It came in under a cloud and swept across me almost like a moving waterfall. Raindrops strike the forest in the distance and you can hear it far off. You know that soon the rain will be upon you as it moves toward you like a wall.

I had a fairly good dose of rain last night, and it was enough to trigger some startling events in the forest. I didn't realize it until morning. I was searching for the nests of Aztec ants and started down the trail to the stream. No sooner had I taken fifty paces when I suddenly came upon a fantastically beautiful display of inflorescences of orchids which had burst into bloom that very morning, in response to the rain. The orchids grew out of a fallen tree trunk which lay horizontally on the ground. I was able to walk right up to the plant and examine all the flowers quite closely. Not only did

I want to get some pictures of the orchids themselves, but a thought popped into my head about a little project that I might try if everything fell into place. I had contact with Dr. Willee, an entomologist in San José here in Costa Rica who studies bees. He informed me that he has had great success in catching orchid bees, a group in which he has a marked interest, by using a specially prepared chemical abstract of the orchid flower. It is a highly concentrated perfumelike material. I believe it has an ester base, which gives off the true odor of the orchid plant but magnified many hundreds of times. He sent me some of this material by plane from San José, and it had just arrived. Here was my chance to give it a try. I brought out the camera, set it facing an orchid flower, and put a little drop of the orchid extract on the tip of one of the orchids. The alcohol in the solution damaged the flower. Orchids have very fragile and tender flowers, and even the touch of a finger will bruise them and make them droop. The alcohol solution did them no good, and no bees came anyway. Apparently, I hadn't put out enough. I took a three-by-five-inch card and put it on the log near the orchid flowers and doused it with eight or ten heavy drops of the fluid from an eye-dropper. To my astonishment, within one or two minutes I detected the buzzing sound of bees around me. At least four or five of these fantastic orchid bees swarmed around the card. I say *fantastic* because these bees are beautiful in their color—metallic, coppery, bronzes, greens, and blues. They are also fantastic in the shape of their hind legs; the tibiae are expanded into flat, curved, triangular plates; and they are fantastic in the length of their tongues. The tongues of some specimens are two to three times the length of the body. Now the reason that these bees are called orchid bees, and that they have some of these structural characteristics, are that the males are responsible for pollinating certain species of orchids. This is a known fact to entomologists and botanists. The bees, I should mention, belong to the

OVERLEAF:
This *Sobralia* orchid served in the experiment with orchid extract, which was used to attract orchid bees.

Orchids abound in the forest around the station. This *Oncidium* was growing on a tree branch that had fallen into the quebrada.

genus *Euglossa*, which means "true-tongue." As I mentioned, the males pollinate only certain genera, or certain species of orchids. The bee lands on the lip of the orchid flower and attempts to crawl up into the tube to get at the nectar secretions. It regularly loses its hold on the very slippery, waxy surface of the orchid lip and, in sliding back down out of the tube, passes against the male part of the flower where it picks up the pollen on its body. When the bee visits another orchid, it transfers that pollen to the female portion of the flower. Thus pollination is effected.

In order to get some good cinema of the bees going about this process I had to entice them into the orchid flowers. The mere presence of the card in the inflorescence of orchids was sufficient, and in some cases stimulated such a frenzy of flower-visiting activity that the bees investigated and explored many flowers on their own. I wanted to get them into one specific flower, the one that I was focused on, so I tipped it up and put a drop or two of the orchid extract down deep into the throat of the flower. After returning it to its natural position, I saw that it was soon visited by an inquisitive bee, and I was able to get abundant footage of the bees hovering about the lip of the flower, entering it, coming back out, and going through the behavior associated with visiting activities.

This work occupied me most of one day, up until about two o'clock, and I didn't stop for lunch. I wanted to take advantage of the sun coming out from behind a tree. However, I found to my dismay that as soon as the sun came out more strongly, not only did the orchid extract seem to evaporate so rapidly that it lost its true effectiveness but also the orchids very rapidly began to droop and wilt. As I finished, the flowers all faced the ground, hanging limply in the afternoon, having spent only one day in their blaze of glory.

6. On patrol for the army ants

A worker of *Odontomachus*. Touching tactile hairs between its outstretched mandibles cause them to instantly snap shut like the jaws of a bear trap.

I decided to go out on my march for army ants and to cover as much trail as I possibly could. While walking along the trail, I was aware that quite a few of the insects here in the rain forest move slowly in comparison to insects in general in the temperate regions. They are much less likely to take flight when approached. They are very seldom seen going through the air. This behavior is probably related to their protective devices, so many of which are based on protective coloration and mimicry. The effect is enhanced by the insects moving slowly in a manner similar to the movement of the vegetation, or becoming perfectly rigid to better blend with the vegetation, or dropping into the litter to be hidden in the sticks and leaves on the forest floor.

The leaf litter is piling up now in the forest. Whenever the wind blows, tremendous numbers of leaves come down. The term *evergreen forest* is rapidly losing its traditional meaning because by no means is the forest now totally green; it may be generally, but individual trees are losing their leaves and showing their branches more and more. The effect of the dry season in this respect is very noticeable.

I proceeded along a new trail. It is a tributary from the waterfall trail, and it was very pleasant to walk along fairly level ground through the leaf litter. The trail was not too badly overgrown, and I could follow it for some distance before it finally terminated against the trunk of a fallen tree. I have been exploring several trails and each one has its own character, and it seems that I can almost select one to fit my mood for the day. The closest trail leads down the river itself. This is really not a trail, it merely follows the river bottom. I think that of all the trails this is my favorite, because there seems to be a much greater abundance and variety of life to be seen along the edge of the stream, rather more than along any of the other trails. Diverging from the river, there is an upper trail which goes to the cut log that I have been working with. And there's a lower trail, which I call the tinamou trail because it's where I ran into tinamou eggs. Then there is the trail going up to the waterfall to the north of the station. This is where the water supply for the station comes, and off the waterfall trail is a side branch. The last trail, which I haven't explored fully yet, is the valley trail, which goes west of the station up the main valley.

As I say, each trail has its own character. The river itself is open so there's lots of sun, stony bottom, and dense vegetation on either side, and I can pay much attention to the birds—larger birds especially, because I can see up through the canopy here. The upper river trail leads through a very nice primary forest, fairly open underneath the canopy. It is similar to the lower river trail, although the lower is for some reason damper

Twenty-five genera of palms grace the Costa Rican forests. These I could not identify, but a name would not add to their elegance.

The tinamou trail. The rising tremulous call of that bird is the siren of the tropical forest.

than any of the other trails. I don't know exactly why this is true, perhaps it has something to do with the soil there. The waterfall trail is steep, and there's always the sound of the rushing water coming through the forest to one side which gives it an added dimension. At the waterfall itself, the water coming down over the rocks presents a very refreshing sight, and there is the coolness afforded by the evaporation of the moisture from

the rocks around the stream and waterfall. The valley trail, at least in the lower portions, is hot; the vegetation is not as dense nor is it as damp as any of the other trails. The branch from the waterfall trail is similar to that of the upper river trail.

I'm happy to report that my trail walking, which proceeded after leaving the waterfall trail for the upper river trail, resulted in the discovery of a marching col-

Hogue at Linguita Creek. By deflecting the water with my hand I can see minute fly larvae that live on the smooth rock in waterfalls.

umn of army ants. I was elated to come upon the column. I immediately gathered up my photographic equipment to try to take advantage of what little afternoon sunshine there was left. It quickly began raining, however, and I had to abandon filming. Nevertheless, I believe that I was successful in tracking down the bivouac of this column. The wag who said that it's easy to walk through the floor of a rain forest never had to trail army ants. Trying to keep up with the column, which sometimes moves in a fairly straight line, is no easy task because of dense vegetation and hanging vines. It is a continual chopping, cutting activity following the column of army ants. One has to decide, too, at the very beginning which way to follow the column because the column contains ants moving in both directions. There are a few clues to help decide and to shift the fifty-fifty chance a little bit to one side or the other. One involves watching the direction in which the booty is being carried; especially in the afternoon one can assume that the ants are in general returning to the bivouac and that the booty is being moved in that direction.

I noticed quite a few ants carrying wasp larvae and several carrying the limbs of katydids and grasshoppers. It is odd to watch the ants working with a heavy, long load like the leg of a grasshopper, which may be six or seven times the length of the body of the ant. Several ants will work together on this project, and they'll each straddle the leg and run along the ground with the leg suspended between them. It reminds me of a mechanical lumber carrier, one of those grotesque, long-legged machines with the wheels at the bottom that carries stacks of lumber.

There's another clue to determine direction. In this case, the majority of the ants, at least ninety percent of them, were moving in one direction, and very few moved against the main flow. Again since it was late in the afternoon, I assumed that they were returning to the bivouac after a daily raid. The third clue I used involved the direction in which forks in the column pointed. Where I first discovered the ants there was a forking of the column. One fork pointed off to the west, and that direction coincided with the other clues, so I decided to follow the train that way.

I consider myself lucky because I had to cut through only about seventy-five yards of forest to get to what I assumed was the bivouac. The reason I was not sure is that the log under which the ants finally disappeared was closely embedded in the soil. The ants apparently spread out underneath the log into a subterranean cavity, and it was very difficult for me to see into this area without disturbing it a great deal. Nor did I want to upset the bivouac because it was my hope that the colony was in a stationary phase and I would thus be able to go back to it for several days and work with the ants. I thought that I might even finally chop out the log to see whether I could locate the queen if there were no apparent emigration of the whole colony before then. So I was not exactly sure that this was the bivouac. I planned to return on the following day, early in the morning when the column would be just starting to go out. If they moved out in the characteristic manner, I would have good evidence that the site was indeed the bivouac.

It had been a rather laborious task cutting through the forest and keeping up with the column of ants. I stabbed myself at least once in the finger with the sharp spine of one of the spiny palms which are so common here. This is a formidable tree. You have to be very careful not to back into one or suddenly turn and jam your elbow against one because they are needle sharp. One- and two-inch spines project perpendicularly out from the trunk of this tree, and they will penetrate human flesh with the greatest of ease. It causes a very painful wound.

It would be impossible for me to take any one colony and go through the entire life history in the

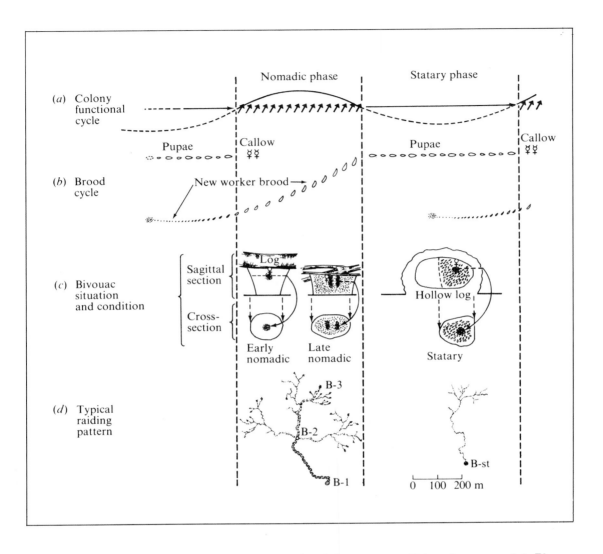

Functional cycle of the army ant *Eciton hamatum.* (*a*) Phases indicated by a sine curve; arrows: large daily raids and nightly emigrations. (*b*) Concurrent development of successive (coordinated) all-worker broods, from eggs (*at left*) to larvae, to pupae, and finally to callow workers (☿ ☿ , *at right*). (*c*) Types of bivouac in each functional phase, indicating typical placement of brood in each. (*d*) Patterns of raiding systems typical of the functional phases; B-1, B-2, and B-3: successive bivouac sites; B-st: statary bivouac site.

amount of time that I expect to be here. This is a task that ordinarily would take many months. In addition, the column might easily move on to other areas and perhaps become inaccessible. So I'm going to try to develop a reasonable story which will give an idea of the complicated life of the army ant. A logical place to start is with the activity of the columns.

I've been impressed particularly with the ability of the ants to make tiny bridges to facilitate moving ants. They seem to make every effort to provide a smooth road on which the other ants can travel. Along the trail in numerous places little clusters of three, four, eight, or ten ants hold tightly onto each other to bridge over some little gap. If a gap can be bridged to make the road better, these ants will fall into the gap, hold their bodies tightly together with their tenacious sickle-shaped claws at the tips of their legs, and thus provide a living path over which the other ants can more easily move. I haven't seen any great distances covered, but I understand that they can bridge over gaps of several inches.

The species which I am discussing, incidentally, is *Eciton hamatum.* It is easily distinguished from the only other with which it could be confused readily here, *Eciton burchelli,* by the fact that the major workers or the soldiers, as they're sometimes called, have light-colored, pale, and smooth heads. The heads of *E. burchelli* are a dull color and somewhat roughened in a manner similar to the surface of the rest of the body. Another distinguishing character of these two species is that *E. hamatum* is a column raider and *E. burchelli* is a swarm raider. The column raiding types of army ants go out in narrow columns and return the booty along these columns. The heads of the columns, exploring ants, move out, find booty, bring back the message, and a single column will go and exploit the booty. The swarm raiders, on the other hand, form a great wave which is a broad path of many thousands of ants, and they bring back the booty more or less individually and converge

By clearing the undergrowth
from the vicinity of a bivouac in the statary phase I
was able to study the colony
close up without being
molested by scout ants.

This decaying log hides a
bivouac of *Eciton hamatum*.
Raiding parties were seen
issuing from beneath it each
morning and returning late
in the day, proof that the
colony was in the statary
phase.

upon a main column. The column raiders are more like the branches of a tree, ever ramifying as one goes greater and greater distances from the bivouac.

The species I saw first is a column raider. At the distance I was from the bivouac, the column reached a width of about four or five ants. The column moved along almost like a stream of water, the ants running very rapidly. Most of the ants were moving in one direction, and the bridging activity seems to have been done by the minums, or the smallest workers. Most of the booty was carried by the medium-sized workers, and the major workers, the soldiers, were running and plying back and forth up and down the column, threatening boldly should the column be disturbed.

The colony which I located was quite obviously in the stationary phase (called statary in the technical literature), being very well ensconced in the hollow log on the other side of the river. On the day after locating the colony, I of course revisited it. My point in going out in the morning and arriving early at the colony was first of all to make sure that it was still there and, second, to try and observe the formations of raiding columns the first thing in the morning. I didn't get to the colony quite as early as I had hoped, but I was pleased to find that there was yet no activity even though it was around eight-thirty or nine, and it had been light for some time. The ants still had not emerged from the log to begin their raiding activities. I suspect that they would not have even become stimulated to that for some time had it not been for my disturbing influence. In an effort to pinpoint where the bivouac was located inside the log, I started cutting away the undergrowth and the leaves and litter around the base of the log. The vibrations of my machete caused great stimulation within the colony, and many ants became active and boiled out from inside the log, obviously intent upon neutralizing my aggression. But, while most of the activity was directed toward this end, it also seemed concurrently to stimulate the formation of raiding columns. It was as if I awakened them to their daily task earlier than they were used to.

One of the things I did was to try and see if I could stimulate the ants to form up a raiding column by dropping prey in their path. I captured half a dozen katydids, and partially immobilized them by pinching their thoraxes so that they would not be overly active and escape. I dropped them in the path of an embryonic column, one that was just forming, and the movement of the prey stimulated the ants to tremendous aggressive activity, biting, stinging, tearing with the jaws. Moreover, the message seemed to be relayed back to the other portions of the colony, and an increased number of ants came off in that direction to take the prey.

I was extremely impressed by the great tenacity of these worker ants. Their tarsal claws, the little hooks on the tips of their legs, are especially adapted for clinging to other ants in the formation of bridges and the like. They are also used like grappling hooks to hold onto prey, which they do with tremendous force. They have a huge capacity to hold and great strength as well. One katydid, several times the mass and size of a medium-sized worker ant, attempted to escape. The ant had hold of the tip of the hind leg of the katydid with its jaws, and at the same time hung onto a margin of a leaf with its legs. In spite of being pulled and dragged along the ground in this tug-of-war the ant held its ground and actually prevented the katydid from escaping. This was all done by one single ant.

The bivouac normally awakes in the early morning, although I observed a contrary situation in my colony. The foot candle light intensity required to stimulate the emergence of such ant colonies has actually been measured. It takes 1.5 foot candles to get them moving. Of course, I had no way to measure light in that manner, but it seemed very dim in the vicinity of the bivouac, even as late in the morning as it was. Possibly there was still

A trail of *E. hamatum*. The medium-sized worker in the center of the picture is carrying booty, the cocoon of some hymenopterous insect.

not enough light to stimulate them to their raiding activity. There appeared instead to be a kind of general disorientation, the activity within the colony seeming to have no purpose or direction. The ants just milled about; singly, in short columns probing out from the main mass, in little groups forming bridges, and in little groups forming separate hanging masses apart from the main bivouac. This general milling went on for some time until there began to develop in the colony some sort of organization. Just how this is effected is a very difficult question, but there seemed to be a message which was gradually sent about and interpreted by the ants. Then firm columns began to develop very short, single probes which went out like the pseudopodia of an amoeba, testing the leaves and the forest floor for some input that would arouse all of the members and send them off into a single directed activity. Gradually, these various probes diminished in number and one became dominant.

In the columns which develop at the very early stages, it is usually the minor workers that act as the pioneers, that go out and lay the trail. I would presume they are partly encouraged to do this by some sort of internal, physiological drive, and also by the mounting pressure of the rest of the colony behind, which pushes them along like subway passengers being pushed along into columns to board a train. They tend to follow the path of least resistance, and, bit by bit, these minor workers find success. It seems that the finding of prey close by is a very strong stimulating factor to the forming up of a major main trunk in the raiding column. The message is sent back by the returning workers which have experienced a contact with the prey, and the booty begins to be carried back along the column. Undoubtedly, this serves to reinforce more and more intensely the strength of the major column. The major column itself consisted primarily of the minor workers and the medium-sized workers, which formed up in tight files in the center. The major workers, or soldiers, followed along later and appeared to be crowded to the outside of the column. Nor did they take a great interest in the raiding activities at the very beginning. But should the column be disturbed in some way, if I were to break it with my machete, then the message would quickly reach soldiers back in the main mass. They would then rush to the point of disturbance and take up their grotesque, characteristic defensive poses, reared back on their hind legs with their jaws spread widely apart and looking very fierce.

OVERLEAF:
The oversized sickle-shaped mandibles identify this as a major worker of *E. hamatum*. The jaws and sting are used aggressively in fending off threats to the colony.

When one thinks about it, this column arrangement makes a great deal of sense. The smaller workers, who actually do most of the raiding and carrying of booty, are in the inside, while the larger, more aggressive ones are on the outside forming a protective flank to the main column. It is similar to a naval convoy with its destroyers on the outside and the defenseless freighters in the middle.

Several days later, I had the impressive new experience of going to the head of the raiding column of the army-ant colony. By carefully following the main column leading out of the bivouac about ten-thirty or eleven in the morning, I was able to trace it up to the point where it began to bifurcate and spread out like a meshwork of fingers, and where the great activity of raiding and ripping and tearing and catching the prey was taking place. It was a fantastic experience for me. I've read about the noises associated with the movement of the ants, the din of insects and birds, but the actual event far surpasses the descriptions that have been written.

I found the ants beginning to divide about forty or fifty yards from the bivouac in a southwesterly direction. They made quite a trail. Curiously enough, they even passed through a hole in the trunk of the tree and came out on the other side. Then they wound down through a little ravine and up the other side of a hill. Then they began spreading out. It was impossible to guess how many bifurcations there were in the line of attack. First two, then four, six, ten, and so on until essentially a solid mass of milling, frantically searching, grabbing, stinging ants climbed on all the vegetation, up and down the trees, across the soil, swept through the litter of the forest in search of prey.

Along with this great attack by the ants came an entourage of animals associated with it—particularly, numerous flies which sat on the leaves or buzzed about. As I approached the front of the column, I could ac-

Caldexia (family Tachinidae), one of the several types of flies that follow raiding swarms of army ants.

tually hear a buzzing and roaring noise caused by the beating wings of dozens of flies milling about over the ants. Very little is known about the biology of these flies belonging to the families Tachinidae and Conopidae. But at least some are known to be parasitic. The ants stir up the hosts of these flies and make them easier to find, at which point the flies can dart in and lay eggs. I noticed half a dozen or so different species.

To the sound of the flies must be added the sounds of jumping, hopping, dropping, frantically fleeing insects, mostly katydids and grasshoppers, insects of the type that can jump. They tried to jump out of the path of the ants and more often than not landed in the midst of another swarm. Eventually, great numbers of them were caught by the ants' jaw-traps. It was like a group of men trying to tiptoe through a field of animal traps. The men may miss them at first, but eventually some will step in one and get caught. This is exactly what happens to the insects. As soon as the ants make contact with the insect, they grapple with it, sting it, kill it, and then they tear it into bits small enough to be carried back to the bivouac as booty. The ants of this species, *Eciton hamatum*, seemed to have a favorite booty, the larvae of wasps. I noticed a superabundance of wasp maggots being carried along the raiding column back to the bivouac. I'm sure that the larvae are an easy target for the ants. In and over plants they come across wasps' nests, and go into them and tear them to shreds. The wasps themselves flee, their defenses ineffective against the mass onslaught of the ants.

Yet another sound and action is associated with the head of the raiding column. Various birds come to feed, some on the ants themselves, some on the insects that are scared up by the ants, and some on the other insects and flies that have been similarly attracted by the prospects of a meal. These are the famous antbirds, mostly of the family Formicariidae, among which I have seen the bicolored antbird, the buff-throated woodcreeper, and

the chestnut-backed antbird, the last being the most common. Antbirds are usually not brightly colored, nor easy to distinguish in the forest, some of them running on the ground, some of them perched in low vegetation. Their noise, their voices, their footsteps, the fluttering of their wings, add to the incredible confusion attendant to the head of the raiding column.

It has been stated, and I believe it now, that the army ant presents the most complex instance of organized mass behavior occurring regularly outside the homesite of any insect or any subhuman animal in the world. How these tens of thousands of workers can main-

A major worker of *E. hamatum* locked onto its prey with its large mandibles. Workers this size restrain the prey while smaller individuals cut it to pieces.

OVERLEAF:
Army-ant workers attacking a large katydid. In a matter of several minutes they dismember their prey.

tain a semblance of order during this frenzied activity of raiding is truly a marvel to behold. Think of how they decide which way to go, of how they maintain a unit, a unified army, as they move over the ground, and of how they can find their way back to the bivouac. Incidentally, I have noticed in the last several days of observation that the direction taken by the raiding column has not been the same, and seems to be moving around the compass. How is all of this activity in the brains of these simple animals coordinated? It is an incredible feat of nature.

There are two aspects of organization within the colony which should be considered. One is how the ants control their activity patterns outside the bivouac, and the second is how the total colony is maintained as a unit —that is, why is there integrity within the colony? Why is it, as a huge family, able to stay together and stay with the queen? The first presents an interesting problem in insect psychology, insect behavior. I'm getting involved here with the language of the ants, their ability to transmit messages one to the other, which is a field that is being actively studied by psychologists as well as entomologists. It is known that the ants find their way back to the bivouac by following scent trails which they lay down themselves. These scent trails are laid down wherever the pioneering ants at the head of the column go, so that the ants which follow behind have some marking to follow. The marking is done by a chemical substance called a pheromone. It is unusually persistent, and the ants, later in the day, follow along the trails to return to the bivouac. There is apparently another pheromone which elicits the defensive behavior apparent when a column is disturbed. It works like a chemical trigger.

The maintenance of integrity and organization within the colony as a whole is a more difficult problem, although in relatively recent years it has received a plausible explanation. The explanation has to do with the exchange of materials again, a chemical organizer within the colony. An exchange of chemical materials between the queen and the workers takes place, a phenomenon called trophallaxis. Essentially, the queen provides a secretory substance to the workers and receives food and labor in exchange. The urge for the colony to stay together, in spite of the lofty hypotheses and ideas of writers throughout time regarding the majesty of the ant, is really a selfish one. Each ant receives a stimulation, and in return for this it performs some service and stays in association with the other members of the colony.

Thus sociochemicals make up the "spirit," the unifying factor of the ant colony. These complex substances are not only specific to each species of ant but are also, apparently, in part specific to each colony. Hence, it is usually impossible to mix members of different colonies; take a number of workers from one colony and put them into another and they will be rejected, much in the same way that human cells and tissues transplanted into the body of another human will elicit rejection. Yet, in spite of this superb organization, it is interesting to note that an army-ant column, whether in swarms or in the column-raiding situation, shows no evidence of leadership. Here the analogy of the army ants to an armed human force breaks down. Each individual in the column seems to possess the ability to strike off in its own direction. The others follow the leader, but the leader isn't one in the true sense. Anyone can take over the task of striking out, and it seems that the direction is dictated as much by chance as the stimulus within the body of any one ant. It has been stated that the field operations of these ant armies fit the principles of hydraulics more closely than they do those of military tactics. As far as I'm concerned, the impression is confirmed by my analysis of the movement of the column. I can stand back and watch them over relatively open ground. Patterns of shimmering eddies and whirls and milling vortices of ants move along, and the first members in the lines are impelled

Close-up of the surface of a temporary bivouac of *E. hamatum*. The workers on the outside are mainly medium sized.

A bivouac of *E. hamatum*. The colony is in the migratory phase and the bivouac is exposed.

ahead by the pressure building up behind them of waves of additional workers emanating from the bivouac. Probably, some fragmentation of the wave occurs in this manner, too. Pressure from behind causes some of the workers to break off into new directions, and the whole mass fragments and breaks up into the broad raiding front.

The following of scent trails by the ants to mark their path so that booty can be returned and the bivouac found can be used for an interesting experiment. To demonstrate it, one can take a number of workers and, by manipulating their path, gradually bring the scent trail around into a circle. The ants, like sheep following a leader, will follow this scent trail around in a circle and meet up with the rear of the column. This does occur in nature from time to time, and there are records by army-ant experts who have seen it. A sort of suicide mill is formed.

I became proficient at following out the columns from the bivouac. I could get down there about nine in the morning and expect the raiding swarm to be just a few feet from the bivouac. I could follow them out and keep pace with the movement of the head of the swarm very easily. The movement is only thirty or forty yards per hour, and it is no trouble to keep ahead of them. This makes me wonder about the old fictional stories of great hordes of army ants killing all animals in their path including men unfortunate enough to find themselves there. The authors of those pulp magazine stories and of some of the books that were written about life in the jungle certainly stretched their imaginations to the fullest. When the ants do happen to raid a dwelling it is quite impressive, but there is no problem at all keeping out of their way. You simply walk away from them. In the forest, I've caught myself a couple of times thinking that I was standing off to the side of the column. I would stand there for a few minutes, thinking or doing something, and suddenly look down and realize that the column on my left and the one on my right have out-flanked me. I have to get out of there in a hurry, which means I have to run through a mass of army ants. I pick up a number on my shoes, some of them manage to get up my pant legs and sting me, but still it is not at all a danger. The chances of any large animal ever being caught and overwhelmed by the army ants is extremely remote. Only the unfortunate insects that don't fly well are subject to the ravages of the raiding party.

After working on the stationary army ant bivouac for ten or twelve days, I discovered one morning that it had moved out. It reached a point where the physiological compulsions of emigration were in effect marked by the simultaneous emergence of workers of the previous brood now mature. The whole colony over a period of a few hours moved from its site. A pile of dry empty cocoons on the ground by the log was all that was left in evidence of its former habitation by over 150,000 civi-lized insects. Their new bivouac station was a temporary one and, even that afternoon, appeared to be breaking down in preference for another site some distance away. So, in a period of almost two weeks, I saw the stationary bivouac phase of the life cycle of these ants, then the breakdown, the emigration, and finally the first bivouac characteristic of the nomadic or migratory phase of the ant. The latter bivouac was in an open place compared to the previous one. Now it was under a heavy leaning log obviously having fallen many years ago against its trunk. The log was rotten, and the bivouac hung in the angular portion of the underside of the tree trunk, in contact with the ground at the bottom and in contact with the trunk at the top.

I saw the bivouac for the first time about one-thirty in the afternoon. There was quite a bit of booty coming into it and the normal raiding column going out from it. About half an hour later, the whole aspect of the bivouac changed. Movement intensified outward in the stream of the raiding column. Where earlier there

were only three or four ants abreast, now I counted six
or seven. It was obvious that another mass emigration
wave was ready to set in.

Earlier in the afternoon, I had traced the raiding
party to its head and found typical raiding behavior,
the same as occurs in the stationary phase and with ex-
ceptionally good antbird activity. More species than I
had yet observed were attending this raiding column.
One of the antbirds dropped out of a shrub onto the
ground very quickly and plucked a katydid up in its
beak, just as the katydid was hopping free of the mas-
sive approaching army. The birds obviously took advantage of the agitation of the prey to increase their
chance of finding food.

An unusual double-columned
bivouac of *E. hamatum*.
The colony is in the migratory phase as evidenced by
its exposed location.

The cyclic processes that go on in the army ants are probably the most important aspect of their biology, and the most interesting and the least understood for the longest time. It took Ted Schneirla, of the American Museum of Natural History, a major effort of over sixteen years to unravel and work out detail of the factors which control the rhythmic migration and emigration phases of their life cycle. Basically, the army ants have two activity cycles in their life. One is the migratory phase, in which the colony is restless and moves every day; and the other is a stationary (technically called statary), or nonmigratory phase, in which the colony stays in one location for an extended period of time. With the species that I'm working with, *Eciton hamatum,* the nomadic phase lasts typically about seventeen days and the stationary phase about twenty days. During the stationary phase, a number of interesting things go on in the colony. Perhaps I should explain what is meant by a bivouac. It's a term borrowed from the army, and seems perfectly adequate. It is a grouping or massing, a clinging together, of the hundred and fifty to five hundred thousand ants in the colony in one huge living ball. It is an enclave around the queen to protect her, and to provide a stable environment for her, and her brood. Now, the bivouac in the stationary phase is always situated in a very well-protected place—inside of a log, for example. During this time, the queen is in the process of laying her eggs and bringing up the early stage larvae. Also at this time existing in the colony are ants in the pupal stage, the third stage in the development of the previous generation that the queen produced in the last nomadic phase. The pupae remain interred during the entire phase, and the signal for the movement of the stationary colony, the emigration, is when these pupae emerge and turn into adult workers. All insects are soft-shelled upon emerging from the pupal stage, and for a few hours to a few days they are in a soft or callow state. It is the presence of these callow workers that somehow stimulates the whole colony to an emigration, and this occurs fairly suddenly. (On examining the original colony site, I found evidence all around the log of empty pupal cases, a large number of them.) It's the presence of these callow workers or new workers in the colony, amidst the other preexisting adult workers, that stimulates them to move. Just exactly how this system evolved and what are all of its implications are other questions. For the moment, suffice it to say that this is the stimulus which sets the colony off on its nomadic phase. Thus, there is a series of cycles, if you look at it in a special way. There is first a greater, functional cycle, which runs on slightly longer than the one-month time period. Then there is a daily cycle. And lastly there is a yearly cycle. Now, this varies with different species. In the daily cycle it is a matter of the ants awakening in the morning, the raiding parties going out, raiding until late in the afternoon, and then, depending on whether the ant colony is static or nomadic, the raiding party returning to the bivouac or the whole colony moving on to a new bivouac. This daily cycle is fairly simple, broken only when emigration comes at the end of the static phase.

The yearly cycle is connected with the production of sexual forms. All of the members of the normal colony through most months of the year are asexual and nonreproductive worker ants. Only the queen is sexually active, and there is no male, the queen having been inseminated sometime prior, as required. Usually, the beginning of the dry season is a period when the colony produces sexually capable, winged male army ants.

During the entire stationary phase, pupae are maintained in the bivouac. It is only when they emerge that the nomadic phase begins. During the period of the stationary phase, the queen is developing eggs. Egg laying is not continuous but goes on intermittently for about one week. On approximately the tenth day, she lays her eggs. The eggs hatch in a few days and the young larvae begin to develop. Also at this time, an-

Empty cocoons of *E. hama-tum* beside a buried log, evidence that the colony has emigrated and in the migratory phase.

other series of eggs are beginning their cell stages of development within the female's body.

As she lays her eggs, her abdomen, heretofore very swollen, gradually diminishes in size. It gets smaller and smaller until she is depleted. This is when the nomadic phase begins. One advantage to this seeming coincidence in timing is the mobility of the queen. She would be in a difficult position for migration in her greatly swollen, pregnant state.

As the nomadic phase comes on, the larvae are developing in size and are carried along in the column to the new bivouac each day. The new workers which have just hatched gradually harden up, and their skeletons become deeply colored. In short, they become fully mature, and join the other workers in the function of working for the colony. The queen also moves along with the colony, with the workers. The bivouac still holds its shape during the early morning hours as the heavy raiding column goes out, but, by late afternoon, it begins to diminish as more and more workers pour out of it. A new bivouac site is selected by the leading portion of the column. Normally after dark, there is a sudden emptying of the bivouac and the whole entourage moves out along the raiding trail to find the new bivouac. The last to leave is the queen with her attending workers. This schedule is maintained for a period of seventeen days, with the colony moving each day (in the case of *E. hamatum*). Finally, at the end of this period, when the larvae are fully mature and are beginning to pupate, the colony settles down to a new stationary existence, usually under a well-protected log.

Three main points may be considered with respect to the problem of the developmental environment in these insects. First is the fact that the temporary nest or bivouac of the colony also functions as a kind of incubator for the broods, and the successive bivouacs of the nomadic phase give the larval brood a series of stable, microclimatic conditions within the colony. They are not submitted to the rigors of the environment, the bivouac forming a kind of protective sac, an environmental chamber around the developing brood. It is these environmental effects which have been studied in the bivouacs, and it has been found that such climatic factors as temperature and humidity are maintained at an optimal level for the development of the army ants.

Another environmental factor to which the cycle is adjusted is the quantity and type of booty, or food. The migrations do not seem to result from local food scarcities, as was once widely thought. The theory went then that whenever the food was completely consumed in an area, the army ants would be forced to move out. This has now been shown not to be true. Instead, internal factors cause the rhythms. Nevertheless, the colony is still adapted toward a series of actions which tend to keep the normal level of food available. In the stationary bivouac, raids go out in different directions each day, and a new source of booty is exploited each time. When the army ants come over the same ground again, the insect populations which are their prey have had a chance to build up again. Throughout the cycle of the ants there is a correspondence between the magnitude of the food-consuming capacity of the colony and its ability to gather food, and the chances of finding more food.

A third and final environmental condition to which these army ants are sensitive is light. The daily routine of migration is tuned directly to day-night rhythms, and so the army ants are perceiving the quantity and direction of light. Though vestigial, they do have eyes, but it is interesting that those army ants which live above ground have much better developed eyes than those subterranean forms which belong to the same group. So they do use their eyes to perceive light. This helps regulate the timing of the movement of the colony during the nomadic phase and also is responsible for timing in the raiding actions of the stationary bivouac stage.

Interestingly, the specific responses to light vary, depending on whether the colony is in the stationary or the nomadic phases. In the nomadic phase, the workers react to the very first morning light and the raiding starts promptly at dawn. Although there is a midday depression, or "siesta" effect, involving a marked reduction of traffic on trails from the bivouac, traffic always continues and the columns are crowded again in the early afternoon. These patterns are very different in the stationary phase, especially during the intermediate days. At this time, the colony response is greatly reduced at dawn and there is a noticeable inertia. Raiding either builds up much more slowly or it fails altogether. The midday depression reduces raiding to a minimum, and in the dry season when the effect is greatest, the traffic often will stop for some time a considerable distance from the bivouac. In contrast, nomadic colonies are able to continue their raiding at all times.

The fact that army ants are predacious is a primitive characteristic in ants in general, and the army ants are morphologically, structurally, and in their history a primitive ant. But they have evolved a specialized and highly involved system of rhythms which control the movements of the colony, brood production, and behavior within the colony. The production of males and females and the founding of new colonies is basically the same in all ants. Periodically during the year, sexually active males and females are produced. However, the typical nuptial flight does not occur. Rather, new colonies are founded by fission, or splitting of old colonies in a manner analogous to bees in swarming. After the sexual brood is produced the colony polarizes, the incipient queens and males being taken away from the parent queen. The callow virgin queens which hatch branch from the colony during the nomadic phase with an entourage of workers. Winged males develop another colony and eventually find these queens and settle with them to mate and foster a new colony.

7. The cecropia ant

The *Cecropia*, or trumpet tree as it's sometimes called (or the *imbauba*, as it's called in Brazil), belongs to a weedy genus that grows up in open places and clearings and is an indicator of the edge effect, or second growth effect, which occurs when a clearing is made in a forest. These trees spring up very rapidly. They have a jointed trunk, very much like bamboo with partitions at each joint which completely close off the trunk internally and divide it up into a series of little chambers. When the trees are small, from about two to six feet in height, they are sought out by the winged forms of recently mated females of a number of species of ants in the genus *Azteca*. The female leaves the old colonies, and, winged, mates with a winged male from another colony. Then she goes off on her own to seek out a young, actively growing

Though considered by some as a weed species, the *Cecropia* is a graceful tree when arching in front of a cloud-adorned sky.

Cecropia tree. She examines its trunk. This is a tree that has one single trunk, and does not have really well-formed branches until it gets to be quite large. She searches over the trunk of the tree and finds a small depression, called a prostoma, or internodal pit, which is located just above the base of the leaves coming out in the main trunk. This is a thin area in the wall of the trunk, and she can easily chew through this and make an entrance hole into the interior of the hollow trunk. She enters one of the chambers in the trunk, and after a few days begins bringing into existence a brood of young ants. She feeds the larvae. The larvae mature, and eventually she is accompanied by a brood of worker ants who then take over the task of keeping her and maintaining the colony. These first colonizers of the chamber expand the nest, they bore holes in the septa or the separating walls in the trunk and expand the bounds of the colony into other chambers. This process of colony expansion proceeds and goes along with the growth of the *Cecropia*. When the tree reaches a height of ten, twelve, or fifteen feet, it may have a very well-developed colony of these ants living in its trunk chambers. Sometimes the ants have an interesting way of enlarging the diameter of the chambers. By eating out the internal tissue of the trunk, the trunk wall then becomes weakened, and under the pressure of the weight of the crown of the tree it bulges outward and forms larger chambers than would be natural for the tree, giving the ants a greater area for colonization.

The food of this ant is somewhat a question. They are said to feed upon certain superficial, glandlike bodies which grow in the velvety triangular bases of the leaves of the *Cecropia*. These structures are called Müllerian bodies. The ants also take honeydew from mealybugs or other homopterous insects living on the *Cecropia* tree. One of the colonies that I opened contained three specimens of a mealybug inside. They had obviously been taken in by the ants, otherwise they wouldn't have occurred inside the trunk. I also noted a couple of individual ants going over to a bug and attempting to milk it in the fashion in which many ants extract honeydew from aphids. Also, in one of the colonies of a reddish species, I discovered a kind of cushiony, brownish-orange material growing inside the chamber. It looked almost as if it might be some sort of fungal growth which the ants were utilizing.

A curious thing happens when any foreign object, such as a passing animal, a human, or the entwining branch of a vine comes in contact with the *Cecropia* tree. The ants actually go into a frenzy and come boiling out of the entrance hole of their chambers. I tapped the trunk of a couple of trees with my machete, and within the space of just a few seconds the entire trunk was a writhing mass of ants actively in search of the cause of the disturbance. Some of the ants will crawl out on the leaves and drop off. If you happen to be the unfortunate one standing under the tree and molesting it, you will soon be covered with these ants which bite viciously and will soon deter you from any further desire to molest their home. This obviously shows that the ant offers a protection for the tree. But the extent to which there is a mutual beneficial relationship between the plant and the ant in making the *Cecropia* tree a true ant plant and the *Azteca* a true plant ant is not fully understood or known. It is probable that when the tree is at a certain stage of its growth it does receive considerable protection from the activities of the ant. I experimented once again by sticking the small tip of a vine onto the trunk of the tree with the colony of ants in it. They lost no time in covering it with themselves and viciously biting it, chewing the edges of the leaves, dragging the leaf down against the surface of the trunk so that they could bring more individuals into action to chew on it.

It is obvious that they can deter almost anything from touching the tree. They use primarily their mandibles, and chew the leaves or chew or bite anything that touches the tree. From the appearance of the tissues of the

OVERLEAF:
The poison arrow frog (*Dendrobates auratus*), a close relative of a species in South America used by Indians to tip their darts.

113

leaf of the vine, which turned kind of an olive-brown color, I suspect that there may be some chemical action involved as well, some exudate from their saliva or abdomen which has a poisonous effect upon anything coming in contact with it, such as the cells of the surface of the leaves of this vine.

I later searched out another *Cecropia* tree, a small one about five feet tall, in the hopes of finding a queen. I bisected the trunk of this tree as far down as I could, and, lo and behold, I found the queen. She was occupying the next to the last chamber at the very top of the trunk. She takes up a regal position at the top of the colony. She's considerably larger, several times larger in body mass and length than even the largest of the workers. Unfortunately, she retreated very quickly.

There is evidence that as the trees grow older the ants do not afford it a real protection because there are other animals and insects which can live on the plant. One conspicuous example is the sloth, which uses *Cecropia* trees as one of its favorite foods during a part of the year, and it goes unmolested by the ants. There are other insects living on the trunks of the trees and these are seemingly able to get away without being attacked by the ants, so it may be that the mutual qualities of this association are valid only at a certain time in the life cycle of either the tree or the ant.

The mimetic abilities of so many of the forest dwellers go beyond description. You can't take anything for granted in the forest. Anything your eye sees is liable to turn out to be something else, and almost all of the interior of the forest is a sham. About all you can ever really be sure of recognizing when you see it is a whole tree, or a rock perhaps, but almost everything else could turn out to be something quite different. The dappled pool of life in some nook in the forest might turn out to be a resting jaguar, or an innocent leaf might suddenly spring to life and become a praying mantis or a dead branch or a green vine or even a shadow; an elongated shadow on the forest floor may turn out to be an instrument of death —a fer-de-lance, a vine snake, or some other venomous serpent. It is always frustrating to me as I walk along a trail to know that there are so many things around me that I cannot see. I'm fairly good at picking up many of these insects that are mimicking innocuous plant structures. The way that I do it, if I can explain it at all, is to watch, out of the corner of my eye or in the periphery of my vision, for anything that is even the very slightest bit irregular or out of place or that moves inconsistently with its surroundings: a dry, brownish leaf in the midst of green leaves; a twig at an odd angle; a stone of a slightly different texture from those around it; a stick vibrating contrary to the wind. Then the trick is to stop and examine it in detail. I often find when I do this that what I'm looking at is not what I thought I was looking at, not a leaf, not a twig, not a stone, or a stick, but rather some insect which makes me open my eyes in disbelief, something alive, some form of animal life that is not what I thought it was.

I'm imagining right now, as I look across my little clearing here across the stream at my wall of green, having some sort of special light source that I could shine onto that quadrangle of visual space. I would like these light rays to cause insects to glow some bright color imposed in apposition to the background green. How many insects would I see in that area of more or less one thousand square feet? If in some way I could strip away all of the vegetation and just leave the insects suspended in space, what a fantastic sight I would see.

I decided that I would try an experiment which would facilitate the filming of the life history and biology of the Aztec ants. I decided that I would try to cut down a likely *Cecropia* tree and bring back most of it to the station where I could keep it under control. I wanted to keep a close watch on it all day long and even at night, and be able to work with it in greater comfort. But I had to get my courage up because these ants are

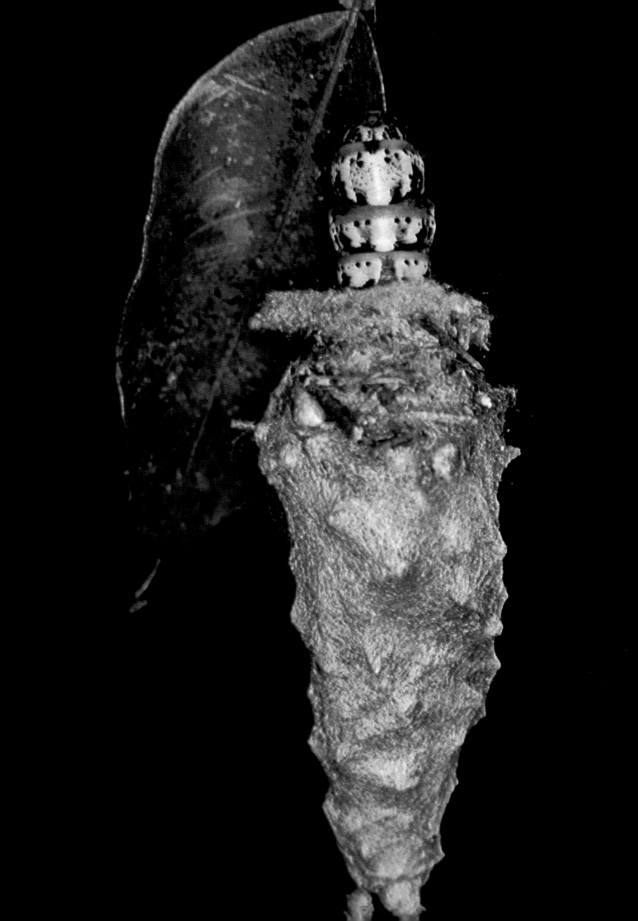

nothing to play around with. They have a frightfully painful bite. Interestingly, they don't actually sting as do most ants, but rather, when they are riled up, they take hold of you with their mandibles and lift their tails in the air and bite with a vengeance. The pain comes from the bite and not from the sting, although I'm not sure if there is some chemical action associated with the bite. At any rate, with such information in mind, I took a long walk down the stream, about three-quarters of a mile, a slow walk. It's impossible to take a rapid walk around here, too many things of interest stop you on the way and there are too many things to get involved with. I stopped off to photograph a brilliantly colored damselfly, of a species that has red at the bases of the wings. I caught this specimen in repose on a leaf with the sun at just the right angle to light up the red color and make the bases of the wings look like rubies as the light shone through them. I also noticed that some bembicine wasps, which are commonly called sand wasps because they dig the burrows in which they rear their young in soft sandy soil, are starting to use the sandy portions of the bottom of the stream for their nesting activities. This speaks of the dryness that is coming over this area in greater intensity day by day. Because they're carrying out this activity, I can expect that there will be continued dry conditions. Dryness has set in, to the point at which each day I notice the water in the stream withdrawing more and more. Whereas it was possible to find water flowing on the surface of the ground for a mile or more below the station, now one has to walk only two or three hundred yards below the stream to find that it has gone underground. The water level all along is dropping noticeably day by day, and the odor of dead organic material, dried-up algae, dead fish, and so forth is very conspicuous as I walk along the drying-up creek. Also, the stream bottom is thickly strewed with dry, crunchy leaves, another strong indicator of the season.

A very large (about three inches long) bagworm, the larval stage of moths belonging to the family Psychidae.

I spotted a number of interesting *Cecropia* trees

which looked as if they might harbor colonies of *Azteca,* but they were too large. Finally, I came to one which was about the right height, about fifteen feet tall, and I carefully walked up to it, trying not to disturb it or anger the ants. With one quick death stroke of my machete I cut the tree trunk in half. As the crown of the tree fell to the earth, I turned and ran. After it had settled, I returned to the tree and cut the tips off all the leaves, stripping down everything except the one terminal leaf. I had brought with me a long piece of string which I tied to the terminal leaf, and cut enough of the trunk off so that I could just hoist the tip of the tree up in the air high enough with my arm to carry it off the ground. As I walked along, the ants were scrambling all over the trunk of the tree in great confusion and great anger searching for whatever it was that had disturbed their home, anxious to bite it and drive it off. I kept the tree away from my body so that I would not contact it and pick up any ants. A few ants did attempt to crawl up the string, but by twanging the string, which was taut by supporting the weight of the tree, I could flip the ants off. I actually made it the whole distance back to the station without being bitten by a single ant, which is quite an accomplishment. Carrying the tree in this manner above my head was a laborious task, to be sure. The blood would drain out of my hand, and the muscles in my arm tired rapidly. I had to stop frequently, every few paces, to rest but finally made it back to the station with the tree intact and with most of the ants intact. I brought the tree around and placed the base in a large plastic container of water, hoping that it might absorb enough moisture to prevent it from wilting.

I was amazed to find that the ants, after a very short time, settled down to what appeared to be normal activity. They gave up their agitation, and I observed them for the rest of the afternoon, just sitting and watching to see what they did. I tried to experiment with the tip of a soft, fleshy plant to see if they would attack it. I tested it against the trunk of the tree. They did attack and chewed it to pieces.

Interestingly, I have encountered what seem to be two species of *Azteca*, a larger reddish species and a smaller black species (*Azteca coeruleipennis, A. alfari*). I have found that a tree which has a colony will have only one or the other species. They do not mix. The tree which I brought back this afternoon contained a very large colony of the large reddish species. I tried cutting a little window in one of the chambers very carefully with my sharpened knife, and did so without being bitten. I even taped in a little glass window, hoping that the ants would not be disturbed if their chamber were at least left physically intact. I discovered, however, that the entrance of light into the chamber caused the ants to go into a great fit of activity, and they set about removing as quickly as possible all of the larvae which were in the chamber. The chamber was entirely occupied only by larval ants which were neatly stuck to its back walls. They were evenly spaced out, a very neat arrangement. The ants quickly removed, one by one, all of the larvae to a lower chamber through a small aperture in the bottom wall of the chamber. I'm going to let it sit quietly all night, and tomorrow morning I plan to carry out some further experiments and open some more chambers and try to locate the queen.

I found a little frog that's fairly common around here—not so much now in the dry season, but much more so during the rains. It's a little tree frog that is dark brown in color but that has wavy, squiggly, irregular, iridescent green lines running all over its body, giving it somewhat of a camouflage effect. This little tree frog is known scientifically as *Dendrobates auratus*, and its common name is the poison arrow frog. There is an interesting bit of ethnology connected with it. The Indians in South America use such frogs in a very special way. The skin of the frog has glands in it which produce a very toxic substance that, naturally, gives the frog

OVERLEAF:
A pool of light on the forest floor. Sunlit spots such as these attract flies, butterflies, beetles, and many other insects much like a pool of water draws animal life in a desert.

121

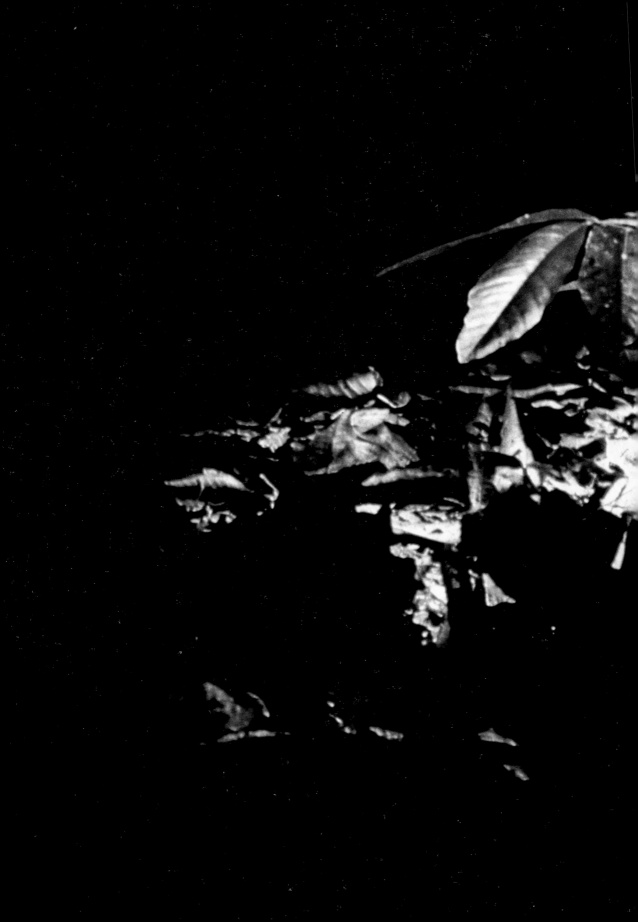

protection from predators. Perhaps the conspicuous color pattern does not have a camouflage effect but rather calls attention or signals predators that this is a species which cannot be eaten because of the poison glands in the skin. Anyway, centuries ago, the Indians became aware of the existence of the poison, and now collect the frogs and kill them by piercing them with a sharp stick. Then they hold the frog on the stick over a fire, and the heat from the fire causes the poison glands in the skin to sweat little droplets of the poison. The poison is then scraped into a container and allowed to ferment. After a few days, the mixture that results is used as a dip for the points of arrows. The concoction becomes extremely poisonous when injected into the body of a vertebrate animal.

Another interesting animal that I encountered today was a bagworm, a very large specimen of a family of moths that normally does not reach great size. This specimen was almost three inches in length. They are called bagworms because they are caterpillars which live their entire lives carrying a heavy bag like a sleeping bag on their bodies. As they grow, the bag is added to and becomes enlarged. It is made principally of silk spun by the caterpillar; bits of twigs and leaves are incorporated into the silk and help to camouflage the bag. These caterpillars are peculiar in that the legs of the abdomen, which normal caterpillars possess, have been long lost in the course of evolution. Only a smooth, pale set of tapering segments remain within the bag. The front walking pair of legs are retained, however, on the thoracic segments. With these the caterpillar hangs very tenaciously to its food plant. In fact, it hangs on so well that by pulling on the bag you can pull it right off the caterpillar before he will let go. The family to which the bagworm belongs is the Psychidae, a word derived from a Greek word meaning soul, breath, or mind. It is also used to denote a butterfly presumably because of its likewise intangible nature. The males in this family are winged, but the females never develop wings and live their entire lives inside the bag that was produced by the caterpillar. If the caterpillar happens to be female, as it grows and matures it pupates in the bag, after spinning the bag shut and fixing it tightly to a branch with silk. The female hatches from the pupa finally but remains imprisoned within its confines her entire life. Only her head protrudes from the bag. This presents interesting complications during the mating season. The male moth, which normally flies and can find the females in their bags by scent, has to insert its abdomen down alongside the female in the bag in order to copulate with her. Her sexual organs are at the terminal end of the body. At any rate, after successful insemination and production of eggs, the female lays her eggs inside the bag and then dies. Her bag then serves her as a place of repose in death as well as during her entire life.

I spent some time the following day again working on the *Azteca* ants. The tree is faring very well, and it seemed to be taking up water from the pail. Even the terminal leaf that I left on is expanding and growing, so apparently it's not going to wilt severely, and the ants have settled down to a fairly normal life in their new position. The little glass window that I put in over one of the chambers is now being sealed off around the edges by the ants. Apparently, they're using little bits of chewed-up plant material as a kind of mortar to seal off the cracks and openings in this piece of glass. I don't know whether they'll cover over the surface and prevent me from seeing into the interior or not. I'll have to wait and see.

The most exciting thing about the activities of the *Azteca* ants today was that I actually witnessed them plucking out the little white glistening Müllerian bodies that grow in the soft tissue at the base of the leaf petiole. The ants seem to relish them, and they pluck them out of surrounding tissue as a farmer would pluck a turnip out of the soil.

8. Parasol ants

While younger *Cecropia* trees seem protected from the attacks of leaf-cutting ants, older, mature specimens like this one are often depredated.

This habit in the Saüba ant [*the Brazilian name for the leaf-cutting ant*] *of clipping and carrying away immense quantities of leaves has long been recorded in books on natural history. When employed on this work their processions look like a multitude of animated leaves on the march. In some places I found an accumulation of such leaves, all circular pieces, about the size of a sixpence, lying on the pathway unattended by ants and at some distance from any colony. Such heaps are always found to be removed when the place is revisited the next day. In course of time I had plenty of opportunities of seeing them at work. They mount the tree in multitudes, the individuals being all worker-minors. Each one places itself on the surface of a leaf, and cuts with its sharp, scissorlike jaws a nearly semicircular incision on the*

127

upper side; it then takes the edge between its jaws and by a sharp jerk detaches the piece. Sometimes they let the leaf drop to the ground, where a little heap accumulates, until carried off by another relay of workers; but, generally, each marches off with the piece it has operated upon, and as all take the same road to their colony, the path they follow becomes in a short time smooth and bare, looking like the impression of a cartwheel through the herbage.

HENRY WALTER BATES,
The Naturalist on the River Amazons.

I went out one morning in April and found myself on a new trail. It is actually a continuation of the lower river trail across the river, and although I had been to the end of that trail many times, I had always turned right for some reason and never let myself go to the left. Had I done so, I would have found some magnificent trails which lead through some nice primary forest. In spite of all the interesting things that are to be found along my usual trails, it does become tiresome going over and over the same ground. It was refreshing to go on into this new trail this morning, and among the new things that I found was a well-developed parasol-ant highway, and then I saw the most fantastic sight of all. Along toward the end of the trail I encountered a small stream which flows under a magnificent fallen log covered with ferns. By turning right at this point and going up the stream, I came to something which I can barely believe—that an insect could have created an architectural wonder. There is a steep, nearly vertical clay bank at the edge of the stream where the stream takes a sharp right-angle bend and, above the level of the water about a foot to two and a half feet, the parasol ants have actually gouged out in the side of the bank a recessed trail. It cuts into the bank an inch or two and is two inches high, so that it is actually a tubular subway system, open only on one side, going along the entire length of the bank some forty feet. The minute jointed feet of these tiny ants marching along—no one knows for how long—have produced this parasol-ant subway, and it is absolutely beyond me to think how this could come about. The trail leads along the bank looking for all the world like the trails which the cliff-dwelling Indians in Arizona and New Mexico made along precipitous cliffs on the mesas of the deserts. The ants have built virtually identical trails, and they're carrying their leaf burdens merrily along.

I find this crude road trail, this miniature Burma Road, to be almost unbelievable. At first, judging from the way in which I've seen other parasol ants operate, I assumed that these trails were made simply by repeated treading and plodding over the same ground. But in this case, and probably in other cases as well, the ants were actively grading and constructing the road by working out small pieces of clay into small pellets. These they removed to one side and in the case of this particular road, built into the vertical cliff, they were actually working horizontally, digging into the cliff in order to extricate the soil to make the groove deeper and deeper and the road surface of the trail smoother.

I've noticed on many of the trails I've watched in the morning that there is very little leaf cutting and carrying. Mostly, the ants just radiate out of the nest. There is some two-way traffic, but not all of the workers carry leaves. It seems that a greater amount of the activity in the mornings is devoted to reworking the trails, especially the recessed trail; which suggests that possibly there is some division of labor among the workers during their normal daily activities.

Eventually, this particular trail leads back into an enormous hole in the side of the bank, a ten-inch hole leading into their nest. It disappears into a hollowed-out portion of the base of a large tree, one that stands perhaps a hundred and seventy feet high. The parasol ants have hollowed out a large nest underneath the base of

OVERLEAF:
Leaf-cutting ants (*Atta cephalotes*) hard at work trimming semicircular pieces of leaf for transport back to the nest where they will be worked into a mulch on which they cultivate their fungal food.

this tree and up the sides of the slope behind the tree to produce by far the largest parasol-ant nest I have ever seen. There are numerous entrances to it, all with very large openings. Again, I feel that I am looking at some sort of primitive human cave dwelling.

Parasol ants belong to the genus *Atta*. These ants have a very peculiar life form. Their nests are constructed beneath the ground in chambers and tunnels which reach a depth of up to fifteen to twenty feet. The nest is an intricate labyrinth of chambers connected by tunnels. All of the members of the colony spend some time in the nest, and the queen her entire life. But the most curious thing about these ants is their method of obtaining food. They actually cultivate and grow special kinds of fungus on a leaf mulch which they formulate and maintain in the chambers beneath the ground. The leaf mulch is obtained above the ground by the cutting activities of the ants. They send out columns which usually follow the same trail day after day so that an actual pathway is worn in the litter on the forest floor, and a series of highways and byways results. At the ends of these superhighways, the ants branch out in different directions and locate trees to their special liking, whose leaves they turn to confetti. Their manner of doing this is also curious. Individual ants go out on the leaves of the tree and start in at the edge of a leaf with one mandible hooking over the edge. Then they draw the mandible through the leaves like a blade, by hooking the opposite mandible in the leaf and forcing the blade mandible against it so that there is a half chewing motion which is carried on in semicircles around the radius of the ant's body. A piece of leaf is liberated finally which will have a semicircular edge where the cutting has been done. The other edge will be irregular, according to the shape of the edge of the leaf. Then the ant picks up the fragments of the leaf in its mandibles, and adjusts the fragment over the back by tucking its head down between the body to get as much of an edge-on grip as possible. The head is returned to the normal position, the leaf is adjusted over the back of the ant, then the ant carries the leaf off toward the nest. Many hundreds of these cutter ants will carry out this activity during the day and night and can strip a tree completely of its leaves. Here they seem to like the leaves of heliconia.

The ants carry leaf material back into the nest, where it is arranged into mulchlike cakes on which the spores of a specific mycelial fungus (*Leucocoprinus gongylophora*) take root and grow. It is the fungus that the ants use as food, not the leaves themselves, so in actuality they are ant farmers, or cultivators engaging in agriculture.

Another incredible thing about the leaf-cutting ants is the long journey which they make from the source of the leaves to the nest. The ants carry their leaf burdens tremendous distances. I don't know the exact measurements of some of these trails, but some are at least a hundred yards long and probably longer. Comparisons between different animals involving loads and distances probably would not be valid. Yet I think it is a point worth a bit of analysis. If you stop and calculate the length of one of these ants and average it out as one-half of an inch, and if you determine that the leaf which the ant is carrying weighs about the body weight of the ant, and, further, if you find the distance of an average trek to be one hundred yards, the ant winds up carrying a payload equal to itself in weight over a distance 7,200 times its own body length. If you carry the analogy over to man, and calculate that a man would take one yard at each step in going 7,200 times his own pace span with a load somewhat less than his own weight you would find that to make a comparable journey, he would have to walk four miles carrying one hundred fifty pounds or more. Add to this the fact that he would have to carry the load in his teeth, and you wind up with a telling analogy. The ants, of course, carry the leaves in their mandibles.

It is not really fair to compare these two animal

Leaf-cutting ants in the process of cutting fragments from a *Heliconia* leaf. The size of the piece is determined by the reach of the hind legs.

payload abilities, because the skeletal muscular systems of the two animals, the insect and the man, function in totally different ways. The ant has a tremendous strength per size ratio over man. Now, this is because the muscles of an insect are on the inside of the body and are attached to the interior of the body walls. Thus they can attach very broadly to the body wall and only a relatively small amount of muscle contraction is required to gain tremendous leverage. So the ant can easily lift its own weight many times over. In a man, however, as in all vertebrates, the muscles attach to the outside of bone. There is, therefore, a limited amount of surface available for the attachment of muscle, compared to that of the skeleton of the insect. The muscles must be narrowed so that there is room for their attachment. They are narrowed into tendons, and thus the strength of the tendon is the limiting factor on the payload which the vertebrate muscles can raise or hold. Consequently, the relative strength per body weight of a man is much less than that of an arthropod, including insects and ants.

Nevertheless, it is an incredible journey that the ants make. It is incredible not only in the total weight which they carry and the distance for which they carry it, but also in the fact that they wear trails in the litter of the forest floor by the treadings of thousands of minute feet. It is incredible because they are able to find their way along this trail by following the scent path, and it is incredible because they communicate with one another along this trail. There is sometimes even cooperation in the carrying of leaves.

The parasol ants will cut all sorts of leaves into the little semicircular fragments that are so well known to the visitors to the tropical rain forest. They will even cut dead leaves, dried, hardened, parched leaves, and even bits of newspaper or other paperlike material that might be lying in their path on the forest floor. They carry these bits of leaves down from the source along trails back to a central nest in the soil. The nest will be fairly shallow if it is a new nest, or as deep as fifteen or twenty feet if it is an old, established nest which has been in one locality for several years.

The amount of leaf material carried by the ants must be tremendous considering the amount of material cut and carried over a period of months. There was a study made here in Rincón by a biology student. He calculated the energy influx into the nest—that is, the new weight of plant material entering the nest per twenty-four hours. He found that the ants carried into the nest approximately 193,000 cuttings of leaves, amounting to 190 kilograms of wet weight leaf material, and 37.8 square meters of leaf surface area. This is a tremendous amount of vegetable material to be entering a nest in a single day. Multiply that by 365 days, and the movement of materials is astonishing. I think this work, however, suffered from some unfounded presumptions, mainly that the rate seen on one day was constant all year. A biologist did find that a large nest, 77 months old, in South America contained 1,920 chambers. It was calculated that during the life of the colony, 5,892 kg (about 2,680 pounds—over one ton) of vegetation had been used in the nest.

The species which seems to be the most common here is *Atta cephalotes*. It's a very conspicuous ant, and its trails are everywhere. As I mentioned before, the continual use of the same trail by worker ants over a period of weeks wears a smooth path on the forest floor that is conspicuously noticeable to the eye, even over a great distance. The ants form overpasses and turnabouts and byways which emulate the freeway systems that men make. They are active all around the clock although mostly in the daytime when the temperature is up. When the temperature goes down at night, they tend to curtail their leaf cutting and carrying.

The most fascinating aspects of the ants is their nest and what goes on in it. The principal fact to remember is that the ants do not feed directly upon the cut and stored leaves themselves. Rather, they feed on a kind of fungus which grows on the leaves. The leaves are chewed and compacted to form a kind of cake or nutrient material on which the fungus is grown and cultivated by the ants. Now, the fungus culture is not acquired in an accidental way. When the queen is produced in the nest and departs for the mating flight, she carries with her— in pockets inside her mouth—a special little pellet made up of a mixture of bleached leaves, little spines and hairs from the bodies of workers and queen ants, and mycelia from the fungus. Queens apparently accumulate this material by combing and cleaning their own bodies in the grooming process typical of so many kinds of ants.

The new queen goes out and forms a new colony by first crawling into a cavity somewhere on open ground. She digs a hole barely larger than herself and

seals herself in completely with soil. Once inside and established in the new nest, she regurgitates this pellet of spines, leaves, and fungus, which begins to grow in the moist air within the nest. She takes care of the pellet, tending it, and pulling out little bits of fungus and applying it to the tip of her body where it absorbs a yellowish liquid which she produces. These tufts are then replaced in what shortly becomes a growing fungus garden, which may reach the size of ten millimeters by the tenth day after the establishment of the new colony. Then the queen begins to lay eggs. She places some of the eggs in the garden where they hatch. Other eggs she lays only to break up. These she adds to the garden, where they serve both as a kind of nutrient for the fungus and as food for the young larvae. Thus, she sacrifices some of the eggs for the establishment of the new colony.

Leaf-cutting, or parasol, ants at work on a *Heliconia* leaf. A short time after this photograph was taken the the leaf was completely reduced to confetti.

The young larvae feed on the fungus and on the eggs, and grow. Finally workers develop from the larvae, and the queen no longer takes care of herself or the fungus gardens. The workers take over this job. No bits of leaves are added to the garden until the new workers begin to go out and forage outside the nest. The first workers are often too small to cut leaves, and only tiny bits of dead fallen leaves are brought in. Nevertheless, the first workers immediately begin to care for the larvae, feeding and tending them. The queen no longer carries out these necessities. However, she does continue to defecate in the fungus gardens, and apparently mold spores are added at this time. The young workers similarly defecate, and the whole fungus mass then begins to grow to a defined, cuplike shape.

The leaf-cutting ants seem to manure their fungus gardens with their feces. It is very likely that the original culture grew on ant feces near the vicinity of the nest. This may explain, in the evolutionary sense, how the practice of fungus culture evolved in the first place. In any case, the fungus is cultivated by the workers, and the colony continues to thrive over months and years, growing larger and larger. More chambers are added, and more broods of workers are produced. An intricate system of underground chambers develops where the queen and the workers live and where the fungus gardens are meticulously maintained.

The parasol ants, oddly enough, are not molested by army ants. I witnessed a column of army ants crossing a trail of the leaf-cutting ants, and there was apparently some sort of interspecies communication which indicated to the two kinds of ants involved that cooperation was required. The army ants seemed to have no interest in preying on the leaf-cutters. The leaf-cutters set up guard stations at the point of intersection of the trails. Guardian ants seemed to take messages from passing army ants, and relayed to them messages to the effect that all was well and under control and that as long as the army ants went about their way the leaf-cutters would go about *their* way and there would be no confusion or fighting.

I did actually witness a battle between a leaf-cutter and an army ant. Curiously, the army ant came out the loser. The leaf-cutter used its powerful mandibles to butcher the army ant, chopping it up into bits and pieces. The army ant's sting seemed to have no effect. This, obviously, is only a single observation. It is a rare occurrence, and probably comes about only through some sort of an accident. The normal situation is for the two trails to cross and there to be no conflict.

I am astounded by the communication systems which must exist within colonies of the ants. How is it that all of the activities of the army-ant and parasol-ant colonies can be so astoundingly well correlated, so well regulated that the colony functions properly, that all the jobs are done, that the colony maintains its integrity as a unit? I have discussed those factors which are involved in the integrity of the colony, the chemical, trophallactic substances exchanged between the queen and other members of the colony. I have also talked a little bit about the scent trails laid down from glands in the bodies of the ants, which explains in large part their navigational abilities. But what I have not discussed yet is the most intriguing of all: how does a colony of ants arrive at a decision?

This process becomes most vivid when an army-ant colony makes a coordinated move. A number of decisions do have to be made. A critical one is the question that is posed before the colony, "Where shall we bivouac tonight?" The colony in a migratory phase must push out from its bivouac site every day and take up residence for the night elsewhere. The following sequence is typical: a raiding column is sent out, scouts go out from the bivouac and practice their raiding activities, and also along the route at a certain time of the day a suitable log, overhanging branch, or other protection is presumably found. It obviously has to be explored and evaluated as a bivouac site for the next day or for that very night. All right, now stop and think of the logic involved in this complicated chain of events which must occur. Whether or not the stages in decision making occur within the ant colony in the same way in which they do in the human mind is another question, but the site first must be found and recognized by a member of the colony, or two members, or many members, and evaluated. Then a decision has to be made if this is going to be the bivouac site. Is the decision made in the colony after the messages are sent back from the scouts, or do the scouts make the decision and send it back to the colony? Here are more than a hundred thousand ants which must all, by the end of the day, embark on the same goal. They must all cooperate in the same decision. Now, who makes the decision, when is it made, and how is it made? Further, when it is made, how is it transmitted and explained to all the members of the colony so that each member knows how to act?

These are questions which I think are profound and of great moment, and they are as yet unexplained. Certainly, bits of information must come back by means of scout ants or the ants which have encountered the new bivouac site. Somehow or other, they've got to transmit this information back to the bivouac, because I can't believe that a few ants within the colony are making the decisions for the whole colony. I think, rather, that some sort of statistical assessment is reached by a large number of exchanges of information, and the interpolation of these bits of information with stimuli and signals from the environment, such as the time of day, the amount of light striking the forest floor, the temperature, and perhaps other environmental factors. Somehow, a decision comes out of the colony almost in the same way that an answer to a complicated mathematical problem comes out of a giant computer through the individual but additive actions of thousands of electrical circuits

The silhouettes of leaf-cutting ants carrying bits of cut leaves run down the trunk of this *Cecropia* tree.

which exist. Such complexity must also exist in the individual and collective circuitry of the nervous systems of the ants.

Now, I realize that I am a long way from explaining what goes on, but from my observations I cannot believe that the queen in her royal position makes the decision by evaluating the information. She can have no way of knowing, visualizing, and evaluating a site which is yards and yards from her. Nor can I believe that there is some sort of group of ants, or council of ants, charged with the decision making and responsibilities for the colony. Yet I think that, when the answers are finally found, they will involve more than a mathematical system with a complicated mechanism giving a relatively simple result.

The whole question of communication in the ants is one which has been studied and reflected upon for a long time. Probably the most popular idea along these lines is that ants communicate by an antennal language of some sort; that is, they talk by touching their antennas. This is an idea which is quite old. The first accounts appear in a book by Huber called *The Life and Deaths of the Indigenous Ants*, printed in Paris and Geneva in 1810. Apparently the ideas about antennal communication originally came from this work and have seeped into the popular literature. There have been some attempts to decode the messages and to determine if they are real or not, particularly in the works of Wasmann and Forel. A language has actually been hypothesized for some species of ants, although recent ideas tend to discredit the notion that there is a complicated system of antennal language in ants. But from my personal observation of the activities of army ants particularly, and in interspecific reaction with the parasol ants, it would seem likely there is some sort of antennal communication, possibly by the actions of the front legs as well. I'm very anxious to look at high-speed pictures of ants meeting one another on the trail to see if they exhibit consistently repeated movements of touch with their antennas and legs.

Ants also communicate with sound by stridulation, although this is not too common. There are ants which stridulate and make a noise somewhat like the distress call of a bird. At the very least, it calls attention to an ant in trouble, and may also have other information to communicate. But I think, in sum, that myrmecologists believe that the most important "language" used by the ants is the chemical language, the employment of pheromones.

9. The aesthetic "I"

I expected to have a very poor day with much rain, but it didn't materialize. Instead, the morning was one of the most beautiful mornings I have spent in the forest. It is late March. I was up early and saw heavy clouds down over the Golfo Dulce bringing me a beautiful golden sunrise. For some reason, the forest was unusually fresh and crisp. I got out and down on the tinamou trail early —probably about eight-thirty or nine. I can't really put it into words, but for some reason everything was different. It was cooler, for one. I read the thermometer about eight o'clock, and it was sixty-nine degrees—probably cooler because of the heavy rains two days ago. I think everything was washed clean and made new. The air was freshened by the coolness and by the moisture, and the animals were stimulated. Fog shrouded the valley

One of the golden skies which make the forest near Rincón such a soul-stirring environment.

floor, and the air had a slight mist in it which gave it a tangible substance. I was able this morning to take advantage of the beauty of the forest more than any time before. I walked past plants dripping wet from the dew and mist, and I saw leaves translucent through their moisture, the sun shining brightly behind them. I saw the bark of the trees covered with moss and, for the first time, lichens exposed to the sun. Everything seemed to be made ready for me. I encountered one beauty after another.

I was able to verify something about the rain forest this morning which has long been written and talked about, and that is the steaminess of the forest. The old idea of the steaming hot jungle is simply not valid. To be inside of the forest is not like being inside of a steaming hot box; rather, it is cool. Of course, you sweat profusely, because the humidity allows perspiration to accumulate on your skin, but the temperature is never very high, around eighty degrees, and there is a feeling of freshness if you can remain still and do not exert yourself. However, a few days ago I saw the steam or water vapor rising off of my shirt in response to the warming rays of the sun. Well, this morning for the first time I saw clouds of water vapor coming off plants in a natural way. The heavy moisture on the leaves vaporized because of the clear, bright sunshine.

Morpho butterflies were out, their beautiful blue wings flashing across the clearings and through the pools of light. A large *Ameiva*, a lizard, suddenly appeared. He turned a little twist or two in the trail before running off into the darkness of shade. I saw a very small viper, probably a very young *terciopelo* ("velvet," the name given to the fer-de-lance by the Costa Ricans in reference to its deep pastel colors) this morning, and the little red frog *Dendrobates granuliferus*. I don't know why, but there is something about the habitat of a certain portion of the trail that is especially suitable to these delicate frogs.

Incidentally, the generic name, *Dendrobates*, liter-

ally means tree walker, and thus applies very appropriately to these tree frogs. I know a curious thing about the poison arrow tree frog mentioned in Chapter 7, *Dendrobates auratus*. Although *auratus* means gold, this particular species of tree frog is not gold at all. It is a dark brownish-black frog with squiggly green lines all over it. However, to a red-green colorblind person, this frog would appear goldish in color. It is very possible that the person who originally named this frog and described it formally in the literature was red-green

Dendrobates granuliferous, a brilliant red tree frog that likes to hide among the thorny stilt roots of spiny palms.

OVERLEAF:
Another of the tree frogs, *Centrolenella.* This species' belly is transparent, and his internal organs can be observed functioning if a specimen is placed on glass.

colorblind. Thus, in all innocence, he gave it this name, and, misnomer though it is, the scientific world must live with it.

So this morning was an idyllic one, and I think I was able to accomplish more in an aesthetic than in a practical sense. I always have the fear that the more spectacular the sight is that I photograph, the more chance there is that the film won't come out right (either I've forgotten to set something on the camera or I'm misjudging the light). It causes me a great deal of trepidation and uneasiness to suspect that I've lost my chance, and I know I have lost it in some cases. This is one element that bothers me about working with photographs; there's always the pressure to make good the exposure and, as a consequence, I don't have the time or the freedom to enjoy the sight that I'm seeing. I feel the same way about keeping notes. I have never been a good note keeper, and I have never had the slightest desire to keep a diary. When I go on field trips I have to force myself to make written records of the things I see and the things I do. I realize it is a very good practice to keep notes, because these records are valuable for future reference. But somehow I can't escape the feeling that making a record of the experience or the object, whether photographically or by writing it down or by tape recording, somehow depersonalizes and dilutes it. The record-keeping requirement takes the pleasure out of it, takes away the personal intercourse that I receive from seeing the sight and beholding it and being gratified by it and being astonished by it. Somehow or other, those experiences that I have had and those sights that I have not written about but have seen with my own eyes at some secret place are the ones which I value the most. Those things that I have forced myself to write about have lost their spice and simply don't make the sweeter part of my memories.

So, in one way, the photographic part of this venture is somewhat unsatisfying. I realize the need for the

camera, the need not to miss opportunities, but I always have the weight of the camera and the equipment not only on my back but on my mind. I would give a lot for a day simply to wander without the pressure to take pictures, to take notes, or to make a recording at the end of the day and simply to enjoy every sight, tasting it, swallowing it, and savoring it, making the most of it.

I encountered a butterfly near an army-ant bivouac site, one which is highly characteristic of the rain forest. The owl butterfly (*Calligo*), so named because on the underside of the hind wings there are two large eye spots which, with their surrounding mottled brown fleckings and coloring, look exactly like the face of an owl. These butterflies are not common but are occasionally seen in the denser, more somber parts of the forest where they

Smilisca phaeota, a tree frog that showed up on the kitchen sink one evening. The species lives near ponds in the forest.

Hogue taking still photographs. The use of extension tubes and the lack of light in the forest necessitate stroboscopic lights.

will flap their spacious, elegant wings. They span some five to six inches from wing tip to wing tip, a large butterfly with a heavy body. Sometimes, after a gyrating sojourn through the forest, they come to rest on the upright trunk of a tree where they may be approached and caught with your fingers if you're very cautious. The upper sides of the wings grade from blue along the posterior edge of the wings to a vivid orange on the anterior edges. It's a beautiful butterfly but one which I could not photograph this morning.

Taking notes is an endless task. I spent a good portion of each evening recording film data.

To follow the often erratic flight of many tropical birds it is neccessary to handhold the camera.

10. The pathetic stomp and shuffle

A caterpillar of one of the tiger moths (Arctiidae). This black woolly bear is little different in outward appearance from its temperate relatives.

Standing around back of the station one morning, I found myself in the midst of a fire-ant nest. These pernicious ants crawled up my pant legs and started stinging me on the legs. I embarked on a perfectly normal reaction. I stomped my feet violently in order to knock as many of them off my boots as possible. To get them off my legs, I engaged my limbs in a wild, scissorslike motion, the while flailing madly with both hands. I kicked my feet against whatever object I could find: the station, rocks, trees, and Andy, the itinerant ornithologist. I stamped and banged and slapped my legs and squeezed the ants down in my boots to try to rub them out. This whole activity reminds me of what might be a new dance, the Fire-Ant Stomp. While it is not much fun, it throws the body into a series of wild contortions and undulations which are rarely achieved in any established and socially acceptable dance.

This brings to mind yet another dance which I think I could add to the world's repertoire. I shall call it the Horsefly Shuffle. The Horsefly Shuffle is a series of rapid waving movements of the arms and hands past the ears with the palm open and then, with an equal number of quick waving movements, back and forth in front of the face and around the back of the head. At the same time, the whole body must be tossed and vibrated. The essential function of this dance is to keep horseflies away from your face and your ears and away from the rest of your body so they won't light on your face and bite it nor on your clothing and bite through it with their murderous mandibles.

The eyes of the horseflies, however, are wondrous things. Seldom does a person get a chance to look a horsefly in the eye. Rather, when he is pestered by one of these seemingly ubiquitous insects, his first thought is to drive it away or to crush it. But if you can restrain yourself sufficiently to take a second when you are being bitten by a horsefly, look into its eyes very carefully and you will see an incredible display. The eyes of most are brilliantly colored. They are arranged in stripes and circles, and contain all the colors of the rainbow. The panoply of colors disappears when the horsefly dies, however. The radiant colors in life are brought about by a layer of water beneath the lens of the eyes which forms a reflecting surface and gives off a variant refractive hue to the different portions of the eye—much in the way that a diamond refracts in different colors of light. But when the insect dies, the moisture dries out and the colors fade, although they can be revived to a certain extent by placing the insect in a moist chamber. The moisture is picked up again by the eye through absorption, and the colors reappear momentarily.

I would like to acquaint you with another persistent element of the forest, one invariably connected with human beings. It announces itself with a swoosh and a gasp, and you can hear it every single night. It is the sound of the plastic squeeze bottle in which I have placed a ninety-five percent solution of alcohol.

I use the alcohol part of the time to preserve specimens, but most often I use it on my legs and on my bites. I continually sustain dozens of insects stings and bites on my legs. One evening I counted over one hundred and seventy. It is a constant trial and completely aggravating. I'm looking forward, with more pleasure than anything else, to getting away from these irritating critters and letting my legs heal up and the itch go away. I suffer repeated fits of itching and scratching. When I put my boots on in the morning my feet are sore and begin to itch and hurt. I pull my pant legs down over my legs, and my legs become irritated and start to itch and hurt. It just goes on and on, and I get sick of it. I'll have to say sometimes I get pretty tired of the monotony of this place, too. I think it is starting to get to me. I'm in a hole in the jungle, and all I can see are green trees and the ground and the sky, all of which engulf me.

I think that being here in this climate and in these conditions, sitting down in the middle of this clearing and looking up all the time and seeing only green vegetation and sometimes blue sky brings on a kind of decay and disruption of the brain that you don't experience in more open country. Maybe this is just a function of the fact that I was brought up in open country. I know best of all the deserts and mountains around Los Angeles. I was always able to move about freely with an automobile or bicycle when I was a kid, and I've always been able to vary my views. But here, in spite of the great diversity, there's still a great uniformity. It's hard to explain. It is a paradox, but it's true. Again, the idea of the green hell prevails, which I never believed in before. But I've been here now nearly two months, and I think there is substance to it. It's like trying to make a living in a bowl of green Jell-O. You try to move, and

157

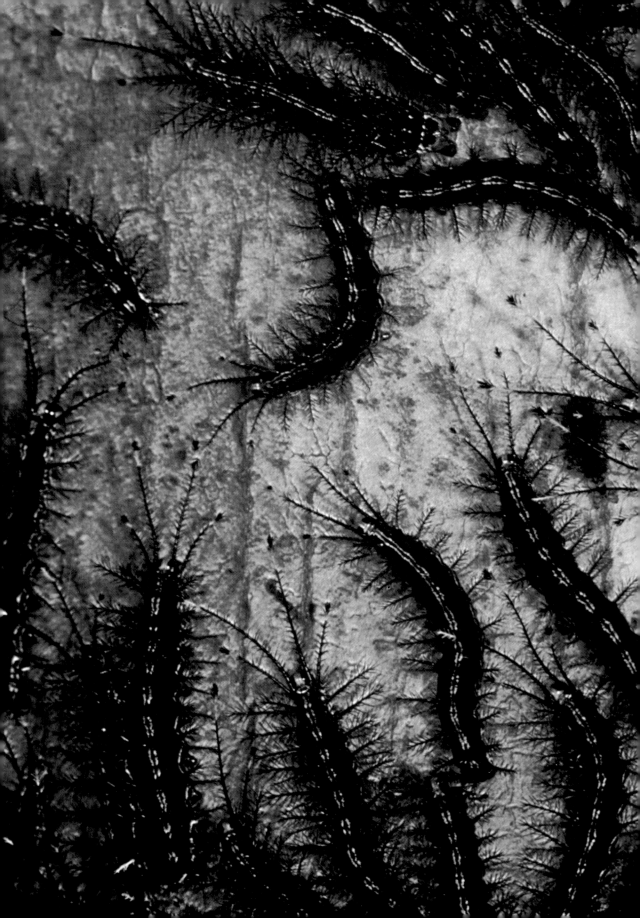

you meet resistance and vibration. Any kind of problem, no matter how minor, holds you down as a mass of gelatin would hold you down if you were trying to be active inside of it. And this phenomenon is gradually working on my brain, so that I sometimes lose my ability to resolve the problems of the day.

I lose track of time completely. It may be nine o'clock in the morning, and as far as I am concerned it's two in the afternoon, or vice versa. The weather pattern is such that from the hours of about nine in the morning to four in the afternoon the sky looks always the same. The position of the sun is sometimes determinable but not always, because of the frequently heavy cloud cover. And the sky is always mottled with clouds. Except for the sun from time to time, there is no set landmark in the sky to go by. So I lose my ability to solve problems, to keep track of time. I can see why the old tropic fever affected the Europeans, the explorers and the colonists all over the tropics. People from the temperate regions simply can't go in and expect to function the way they do in their own environment.

The local population, on the other hand, is adapted to this unremitting sameness. They have slowed their pace, and I actually think that time moves at a different rate for them than it does for those of us from the northern regions. To them, I think, each day is like every other day—and it nearly is, in terms of the length of the day. Moreover, the seasonal changes are not great. There is the change from the dry to the wet season, but then, again, it's a relative change here in the forest. And there is no great transition. So they are adapted to it and they function at their own pace and in their own manner. They are perfectly happy with that. A person like myself, transplanted from his environment to this one, is ill-adapted to the situation here. In forcing myself to adapt and in trying to function here, I constantly run into conflicts. Just yesterday, the pressure built up to a point where my capacity to think broke down.

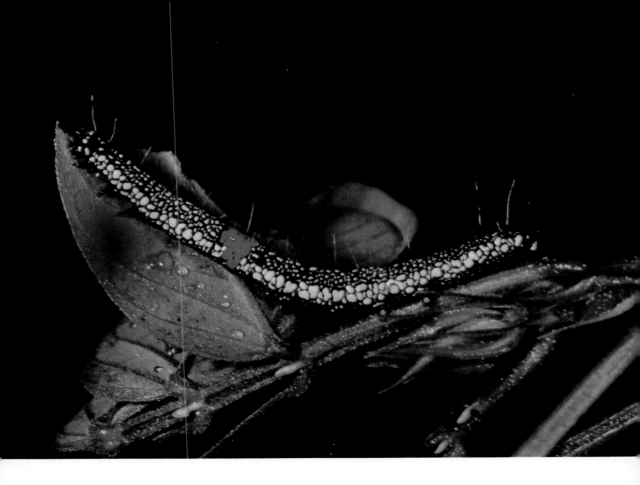

It was such a muggy, warm, sweaty afternoon. I just gave up for the day and went to bed early to get a good night's sleep. But habitually I wake up early in the morning, about three or four, and cannot go back to sleep no matter how hard I try. For some reason, it is impossible for me to get a complete night's sleep here. I can't explain it. It is cool in the evening and comfortable. Perhaps the night sounds of the forest are audible to me, or perhaps I have a subconscious fear of being lost here; yes, a subconscious block against giving myself up completely to this place.

I know people from the United States who are compelled by efficiency and proficiency and used to maintaining time schedules. Were they to come here and try to duplicate their organized lives, I am quite sure that, in short order, they would despair and be completely lost and would leave. They wouldn't be able to take it.

An unidentified caterpillar. The species' bright markings may signal a predator that the species is bad tasting.

I have had enough experience in the tropics of both the Old and New World to be aware of this tropical ennui, this jungle fever. It frustrates me, but it doesn't come as a surprise and I can take it a little bit better, perhaps, than most.

But one of the things that continues to drive me mad is the fact that I'm constantly scratching, a necessity dwellers in the temperate areas can't appreciate. Not a day passes without a few more bites. I get bitten severely around the backs of my legs by little horseflies, for example. A rather charming symptom that goes along with their bite is that itching doesn't develop until the next day. You develop raised bumps shaped like little volcanoes with peaks on them, and they itch severely. They itch to a point where you can't stand it any longer. And so every night—and this may contribute to my restless nights—I wake up with an itch that needs to be scratched. Alas, the scratching is not a satisfying scratching, it is an agonizing scratching that does no good. On the contrary, it makes things worse, but you can't resist and have to scratch. And so you inflict torture upon yourself by trading a fraction of a second of ecstatic pleasure in the scratch for minutes of agonizing, painful itching that goes well beyond the relatively demure itch of a simple mosquito bite. Fortunately, I have some salve that I keep beside my bed for just these emergencies, which come nightly. It contains a skin anesthetic, as well as some antihistamine. I use this salve on the skin, and within a few minutes the itching is gone and I usually can go back to sleep for a little while.

I'm coming to realize the answer to a question I have had in my mind for a long time, and that is, Why do human beings have fingernails? It is probably an adaptive characteristic that evolved with man living in the forest, where he is subjected to bites and skin parasites such as ticks and chiggers. Fingernails are essential in removing these parasites. I've used mine many times, along with my fine forceps, in removing chiggers and ticks and other parasitic arthropods which attach themselves to the outside of the skin. I think also that the very act of scratching is one that is beneficial in some way. The itch brings your attention to the fact that you have a parasite attached to you or that you have a bite of some kind; then it can be removed by using fingernails. Thinking back in time, if I were a primitive resident here in the forest I would use my fingernails in this way to remove the parasite and eliminate the symptoms. So possibly this is a primary function of our bladelike fingernails. I would have to refer this question to Desmond Morris, and find out what he says in *The Naked Ape* about the adaptive significance of fingernails.

I'm getting more tired every day, and it's a little bit harder to do my duty. I have been spending some time away from the army ants, getting back to some insects that accumulate at the 15 watt ultraviolet night light I have erected. I discovered a nice big stinkbug with pointed shoulders, about an inch long. He was cleaning his antennas in a very curious manner. These stinkbugs really stink. They have two large glands, one on either side of the body at the base of the abdomen, which give off a very strong odor when the bug is disturbed. It is one of the few living creatures that does have a detectable odor here in the rain forest. But you have to agitate them to get them to give it off. The cleaning actions that a lot of insects perform, incidentally, are quite important. Everyone is familiar with the way in which a house fly behaves when it is at rest, rubbing its forefeet together, like someone washing his hands, rubbing the wings through their hind legs and the forelegs around the eyes, and so forth. These are not just nervous movements of the insect but necessary actions related to body function. The sense organs of an insect are located all over the body exterior, being concentrated largely on the antennas and on the feet. For sense organs to function properly they must be cleaned, and freed from dust particles, foreign chemicals, or dirt—anything which

OVERLEAF:
View from the front door of the station. From this vantage point toucans, parrots, scarlet macaws, swifts, and a host of other exotic birds may be observed.

163

would interfere with the reception of chemical substances, touch, or vibrations. Hence, insects are continually going through these cleaning movements which are expressly for the purpose of rendering the surfaces of the sense organs clean and in good working order. It's like blinking or blowing your nose.

I did something today that I've been wanting to do for a long time. I had read that people who live here have long known of a secret supply of drinking water in the forest. If you don't know about it, you can die of thirst in the midst of plenty. Inside the giant climbing woody vines that grow so abundantly throughout this forest, there are tubes full of water. If, as I did today with my machete, you slice through the vine, making a clean cut on an oblique, then make another cut two or three feet higher, the water will soon collect at the end held down. It will drip down in a steady stream, sufficient to quench your thirst. If you make only one cut, the water won't flow. The second cut above allows air to enter as the water flows out of the other end. I must admit that I was somewhat surprised when I tried it today and it actually worked.

I sat reflecting on a group of caterpillars for a while. How many millions of caterpillars there must be in this forest, or even in just one square mile of it, all chewing and chomping on some kind of leaf or another and going through their metamorphic process! It is also interesting to reflect upon the fact that these animals represent a totally different form of life from the adult butterflies or moths which they will become. So the kind of lives of insects here in the forest can be multiplied by two, because the metamorphic process of insects results, at least in the higher forms of insects, in two creatures with entirely different aims in life and entirely different processes of living. The larval, caterpillar, grub, or maggot stage is dedicated to the task of consuming food matter and processing it into protein and fats and reserve tissues which will be used by the adult insect. The adult

This mass of caterpillars (*Hylesia*, family Saturniidae) stunned me by jumping in unison at sharp noises directed at them. Mass grouping coupled with this behavior seems to ward off parasites.

insects often do not feed; those that do, however, take mainly an energy source, the sugars from nectar or similar fluids, which they use to make their muscles active so that they can disperse and fly. The main objective of the adult phase is reproduction. So here are two animals in one. Throughout the forest for every one kind, one species, of higher insects, you can get two forms. It is like doubling diversity.

11. The ant and the caterpillar

Walking down the Rio Agua Buena, I came across an uprooted tree which had fallen across the stream. It had fallen recently, probably in the last year or so. Although it is lying on its side across the stream bed, it is not dead and is putting up shoots out of the trunk; and these shoots are growing very rapidly—they've grown about six or seven inches in the last couple of days. But on the tips of these shoots is a most incredible creature. There is a little caterpillar of a metal-mark butterfly about three-quarters of an inch long, green in color, rather flattened and sluglike, with poorly developed legs. The sides of the body are lobed out flat and have a little fringe of hair, so they can press themselves close to the stem of the plant. Right behind the head on the first thoracic seg-

Monacis bispinosus workers tending the caterpillars of a riodinid butterfly. A pair of glands producing a substance sought by the ants is located at each end of the caterpillar's body.

ment are two little horns that are brown and sharp on the end and project out. The head is dark brown.

The reason that I must describe the caterpillar's detail is because I would describe the stem of the plant beneath the leaf in precisely the same way. The caterpillars are a perfect mimic for the growing soft stem tips of this tree. I do not know the name of the tree—I don't know the name of ninety-nine percent of the trees here—but the stems below the leaf are swollen out in such a way that it would appear to be the body of a caterpillar. The axillary bud, the little shoot which occurs in the angle between the base of the leaf and the stem, is simulated very closely by the horns behind the head of the caterpillar. You have to look a long time to see the caterpillars on the growing shoots.

Now, this is only half of the story, however, for you can be aided in finding such caterpillars by simply watching the actions of numerous ants, members of a species which run wildly up and down the stems and crawl all over the caterpillars (*Monacis*). On closer inspection, you can easily see that the ants are actually tending the caterpillars; that is, they are crawling over them and palpating them and taking what I presume is a honeydewlike secretion from two conspicuous little glands on the segment next to the last at the end of the body of the caterpillar. The ants are eagerly drinking this secretion from the glands, and are running wildly about probably looking for more caterpillars. It looks almost as if the ants were engaged in an afternoon ice-cream social.

Now, if I disturb the plant, brush my hands across it, the ants become wildly enraged and race all over. As yet I haven't been bitten or stung, but I expect I would be if I allowed the ants to contact my skin. What I think I'm observing here is another example of a symbiosis, the living together of two different organisms for mutual benefit. Evolution has produced this system whereby the caterpillars make available to the ant a secretion which the ants relish. The ants in return—not consciously, of course, but through an evolved strategic behavior—protect the caterpillars from such potential predators as birds and mammals.

This is not a unique occurrence. There is a very famous example of ants and caterpillars which function in this manner in Europe. There is an ant there, *Myrmica rubra*, the workers of which find the mature larvae or caterpillars of a blue butterfly, *Maculinea arion*. They will spend up to an hour licking the glands of the caterpillar. Afterward, the butterfly caterpillar suddenly bunches up its body. The ant responds to this by picking the caterpillar up and carrying it to the ant's nest. Then comes the payoff: in the nest, the caterpillar feeds upon the larvae of the ants. It would seem that the caterpillars are taking advantage of the ant here, but actually they consume only a small number of ant larvae, and the ants, for their part, have been treated to a very special food which may possibly be an essential portion of their diet.

My ant-caterpillars here in Rincón have the capacity to change their color to some extent. When resting on the young shoots and green stems of the actively growing plant they are green, matching the color of their background. But when they march down the trunk of the tree they take on a mottled brownish-green hue, which mimics the color of the bark.

The ants which are tending them do not, after all, seem to be very closely associated with the caterpillars. I doubt whether there's a true case of obligatory symbiosis here, as in the case of the ants in Europe. Nor do these ants pack much of a wallop; they do get excited when you disturb them but don't sting enthusiastically, which probably means that they have less of a protective role in behalf of the caterpillars than I thought. Also, I noticed the same kind of ant feeding on exudates from trees and other liquid sources in the forest. It's possible that they are just taking advantage of the presence of

OVERLEAF:
Extreme close-up of two worker *Monacis* ants feeding simultaneously at the anterior and posterior glands of the riodinid caterpillar.

171

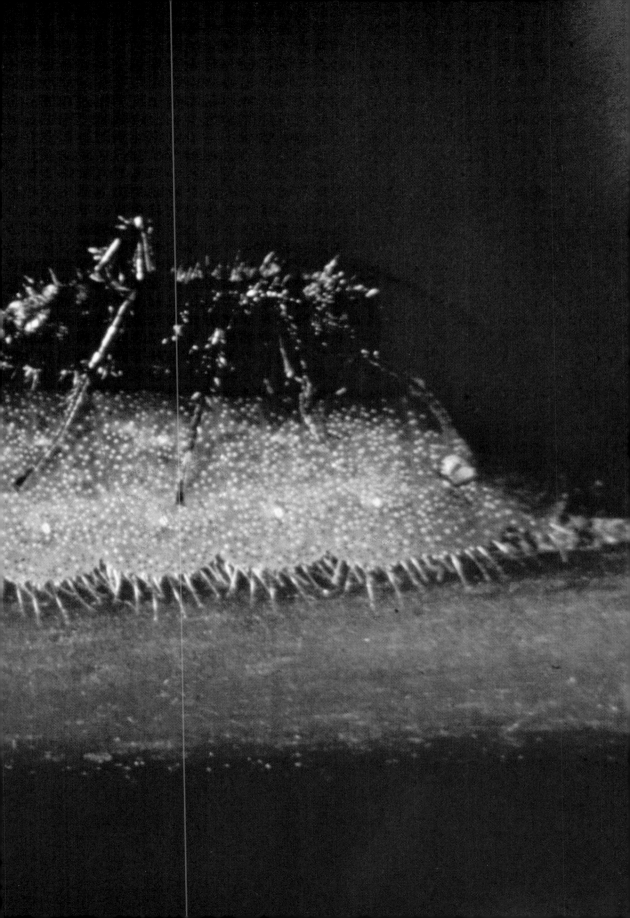

these caterpillars and have taken them over for their own. The ants definitely do not carry the caterpillars away to their nest or anything of the sort, so there's no comparison with the European ant-caterpillar relationship. The ants seem to be doing just the opposite. By the palpitating movements of their antennas and by their general agitation, they almost seem to be trying to hypnotize the larvae to stay where they are. Rather than letting the larvae crawl away, the ants seem to use whatever assuaging powers they have to keep the caterpillars situated so that they can continue to take advantage of the secretions from those two little glands on the abdomen.

Many insects feed on fluids of one kind or another. A wide variety have especially adapted mouth parts for feeding on liquid substances in nature. The range of liquid substances is great. Flies, particularly, exploit the liquid source of food in nature. I ask my entomology students if they can think of liquid sources, and usually they can think of only three or four. Nectar is an obvious one. Many insects feed on nectar, which is a liquid, sugary substance produced by flowers. Then there are the saplike secretions from trees avidly exploited as food by many kinds of insects. In addition, there are the secretions and exudates of plants which are given off under pathological conditions, either as a result of a wound or scar on a tree, a broken branch, or a torn leaf. Often, insects come to the fresh exudate. But others delay imbibing until the exudate has fermented or has changed its chemical composition by decay in some way. Another major source of liquid diet to insects is blood —not only vertebrate blood, but also the blood of other insects and invertebrates. Yet another source of liquid food for insects in the forest is the droppings and leavings of animals, particularly of birds. Such droppings on leaves usually contain a high amount of moisture, or, if dry, the rain can easily rehydrate them, producing substances rich in nourishment and available to these

insects. Rainwater can similarly create a source of food if it dissolves other substances. For example, the water that collects in the flower bracts of plants like the heliconia or leaf axils produces a soup or solution which the insects drink.

While on the subject of exudates, I want to tell you about a very unusual tree. A number of them grow here, especially up on the slopes. The tree is unusual in that it produces a white, milky sap; indeed, it is more like true milk than sap. This is the milk tree, *Brosimum utile*,

Monacis bispinosus feeding on exudates at the posterior of this riodinid caterpillar. The symbiotic relationship between the two insects is not known.

This passion flower (*Passi-flora vitifolia*) twines along the forest floor, rarely climbing higher than a man can reach. It is pollinated by hummingbirds.

called *lechero* ("milkman") in Costa Rica. It is a very large tree, one hundred feet or more in height and maybe six feet in diameter. Although it has large, leathery leaves, the flowers are minute. They are white, and bloom between November and January. When the tree is cut or slashed with a machete, the bark opens up and out comes a copious flow of creamy, milky latex which is quite sweet and pleasantly flavored especially when it's first taken from the tree. After the sap has been exposed to the air for a while, its taste turns a little bitter and becomes chalky—something like milk of magnesia. Within a day or so, it curdles into a kind of chicle or gumlike substance. The fresh milk can be used in coffee, and tastes exactly like good cream. It can even be whipped, and if you flavor it with sugar and vanilla extract, it can be passed off as ordinary cow's milk. I have read that the milk has even been used in other countries to make cheese. However, the milk is not foolproof, for I'm told that dogs, cats, and other animals can tell the difference and they won't drink it. The tree, incidentally, was first described by Alexander von Humboldt, one of the early explorers of the New World, who reported its use in the diet of slaves brought to the north coast of Venezuela.

12. The tropical tropics

The Osa Peninsula from a plane about 1000 feet in altitude. The dense primary forest sweeps away to the horizon as an unbroken carpet of plush green.

What is the definition of the tropics? To explain this one has to become involved in a number of considerations. There's no simple, one-line definition. First of all, we have what we call the celestial tropics or the astronomical tropics, which is the zone that is determined geographically by the position of the sun in relation to the north-south latitudinal bands of the Earth. The tropics, geographically speaking, constitute a broad latitudinal zone between north and south latitudes twenty-three and a half degrees. This is the *zona torrida*, the hot zone of the ancient writers. The specific latitudes that are chosen to delineate this zone are defined as the highest latitude reached by the sun's perpendicular rays during its north-south migration each year. When we talk about tropical regions, we must also talk about climate. Within the sphere of tropical climate we have two subdivisions: the first is altitudinal climatic changes, and the second is the latitudinal climatic pattern controls. The first is fairly simple to define, and it is based on the regular progressive decrease in temperature with an increase in altitude or elevation. Wherever you are in the world, there is a decrease in average air temperature of approximately one degree Centigrade for every one hundred and fifty meters' rise in elevation. There is only one altitudinal zone in the tropics that can be called tropical, and this includes the lowest elevations from zero to about one thousand meters, the lowlands or the *tierra caliente* as they call it in Spanish. These are the true tropical zones within the tropics, because it is at these low elevations that the temperature is high enough to support vegetational types of the rain forest and therefore high enough to be considered tropical in the usual sense.

Latitudinally speaking, the world's climatic patterns are mainly controlled by movement of the thermoequator. This is a line which would be drawn around the surface of the earth on any particular day which would be exactly beneath the sun. This is the so-called line of fire which moves north and south as the sun appears to move north and south during the progression of the seasons. Now, how is this thermoequator important in determining a tropical area? If you look at the map, you will see that there is a tremendous amount of ocean in relation to landmass in the tropics, so the air is heavily laden with moisture. As the thermoequator causes this air to rise, it cools and condenses, and precipitation follows. Thus, in the tropical zones—the torrid zones beneath the thermoequator—we find a very high amount of rainfall. We can say that high temperature and high rainfall are the two forces that define what we mean by *tropical*. In the tropical regions, the temperature never goes down to freezing, so plants can grow all year round. The temperatures rarely even reach forty or fifty degrees; usually the minimum is sixty degrees Fahrenheit, the maximum rarely over ninety or ninety-five degrees, so this is a region of even, high temperatures. Rainfall in the true tropical areas is also always high, and may go as high as four or five hundred inches in some of the rainiest parts of the world. Usually, a rainfall of one hundred to one hundred forty inches is required to meet the definition of a tropical zone. It is very common to find in many areas of the tropics rainfall of around two hundred inches.

Thus, the word *tropic* refers to the true geographic zone around the belt of the Earth. The adjective *tropical* is used to refer to the lowland hot rainy climatic regimen that occurs within certain portions of the geographic tropics.

In the tropics rain falls during a fairly definite season, and this is caused by the movement of the thermoequator north and south. As the thermoequator moves north—let us say, coming over Costa Rica—the moisture-laden air is caused to rise and loses its moisture, and precipitation occurs. In Costa Rica this happens with a slight lag in June, July, and August, the rainy season in this part of the world. With the rainy season, of course, there is, conversely, a dry season, which generally occurs between January and May on the maximal retreat of the thermoequator. Winds pass over the land without dropping their moisture unless they hit high mountains.

There is a curious thing about the rainy season in areas of the tropics somewhat north or south of the true Equator, and this is that there is often a short dry season during the months of July and August when one should be right in the midst of the rainy season. In Spanish, the word *verano* refers to the dry season or the summertime, and the diminutive form, *veranillo*, is used to describe this short dry season occurring in the midst of the rainy season.

I would like to say a little bit about the climate here

at my station near Rincón. This is of course a tropical climate. The temperatures here are continually high. The mean highs and lows range only a few degrees throughout the year. I should mention that there is no good climatic record for this specific locality, and I rely on the records which are kept at Golfito, about twenty-five miles from here on the east side of Golfo Dulce. But I can judge pretty well what the conditions here are by the conditions there. Temperature stays high with very little fluctuation but does not reach great extremes. The over-all mean temperature here would probably be around eighty degrees Fahrenheit with average minimal temperatures running about seventy degrees and maximum temperatures around ninety degrees. Hence we have about a twenty-degree fluctuation. At night it gets somewhat cooler during the dry season, because the humidity is lower and heat can escape from earth at the end of the day more readily. My elevation is about thirty-five or forty feet above sea level. Because of the curious geography of Central America the isthmus is very narrow in this area. Rincón receives moisture-laden winds from the Atlantic slope a great deal of the time, although it is located on the west coast of Costa Rica. Thus there is more opportunity for moisture to come than would be true farther north along the coast, where there is a sort of a rain shadow as a result of the high cordillera of mountains running through the center of Costa Rica. This cordillera drops off in elevation considerably north of here. There is thus a pathway across the isthmus for these winds, which are able then to bring in moisture-laden air, and precipitation is quite high.

During the year 1965, someone made a few measurements of rainfall at Rincón, and the total rainfall for the year was approximately one hundred sixty-two inches. This is thirteen feet of water. Now, I know that the rainfall here does go as high as two hundred inches, which is a lot of water. The rainy season here, too, is also quite long, and probably lasts about an

This vine, belonging to the philodendron group, has leaves of two shapes. As the plant grows the small heart-shaped leaves appressed to the tree trunk assume suddenly a large, elongate form and spread away from their support.

average of nine months. Thus we have a short dry season running from about January to March. Right now I'm here in the midst of the dry season. There is a *veranillo* expected sometime between July and September, but many years it simply does not materialize and rain continues to fall throughout the rainy season. The number of days with rain in 1965 was one hundred seventy-one. The rainfall pattern is one of gradual ascendance. The rains come on fairly gradually in March and then progressively, as each month passes, becoming heavier and heavier until a zenith is reached in October and November, when the rains may be torrential. Then there is a fairly sharp drop-off at the end of December and during January, and we're into the dry season again.

The canopy of the wet forest at Rincón. Tall emergent trees can be seen thrusting their crowns over their neighbors.

13. Diversity

The different kinds and varieties of organisms in the tropics far exceeds in number the diversity of organisms in the temperate zones and higher latitudes. The old idea that life is more abundant in the tropics has been questioned by some biologists. But I don't think there is any question that life is considerably more varied here. A passage from "Evolution in the Tropics" (*American Scientist,* vol. 38, 1950), by T. Dobzhansky sums this up poetically:

> *Becoming acquainted with tropical nature is, before all else, a great esthetic experience. Plants and animals of temperate lands seem to us somehow easy to live with, and this is not only because many of them are long familiar. Their style is for the most part subdued,*

A cup fungus (*Peziza?*). A simple life form but rivaling the higher in beauty of form and color.

delicate, often almost inhibited. Many of them are subtly beautiful; others are plain; few are flamboyant. In contrast, tropical life seems to have flung all restraints to the wind. It is exuberant, luxurious, flashy, often even gaudy, full of daring and abandon, but first and foremost enormously tense and powerful. Watching the curved, arched, contorted, spirally wound, and triumphantly vertical stems and trunks of trees and lianas in forests of Rio Negro and the Amazon, it often occurred to me that modern art has missed a most bountiful source of inspiration. The variety of lines and forms in tropical forests surely exceeds what all surrealists together have been able to dream of, and many of these lines and forms are endowed with dynamism and with biological meaningfulness that are lacking, so far as I am able to perceive, in the creations exhibited in museums of modern art.

A number of more precise approaches have been made to compare the diversity in the temperate zones with diversity in the tropics. The number of species of butterflies in all of North America, for example, is around six hundred. On the island of Trinidad or in a comparably small area in the tropical rain forest of America, it is possible to find almost an equal number of species of butterflies. In this area around Rincón there may be three hundred different kinds of trees, 1,200 species in Costa Rica. In all of North America, the number of trees, including the conifers, is far below that number. The number of species of mosquitoes in North America is around a hundred and eighty; while in Costa Rica, which has a land area approximately equal to San Bernardino County, California, there are a greater number of mosquitoes. You can take almost any group of organisms and say the same thing. Diversity in the tropics far exceeds that of higher latitudes.

I have found a number of different hypotheses about diversity in the tropics. One is the time theory,

which assumes that all communities in nature tend to diversity in time. Therefore, the older the community is, the more species it will contain. The tropical rain forest certainly is a very old community. Evidence shows the existence of tropical rain forest types millions and millions of years ago. Vegetation, which in floristic composition closely resembled the modern rain forest, date from the Cretaceous period. And in the not too distant geological past, tropical rain forests extended over a much wider range than they do today. Within these areas, evolution, adaptation, and speciation have been adding continuously to the diversity of life. In the

OVERLEAF:
Caterpillars of sphinx moths are usually identified by the conspicuous posterior horn. This is a species from a tree in the quebrada.

191

A pair of "eighty-niners" or "ninety-eighters" (*Callicore* sp.) depending upon which way they are facing.

A colorful tiger moth of the family Arctiidae. This specimen is resting on a white sheet hung behind an ultraviolet light to attract night-flying insects.

This undetermined species
of moth belongs to a very
primitive family, Hepialidae.
It was fairly common at
Rincón.

temperate and in the arctic areas, the biota has suffered great changes in climate and great numbers of extinctions, such as during the glacial epochs, which annihilated communities and reduced the number of species.

There is another theory that the more heterogeneous and complicated a physical environment is, the more complex the plant and animal community supported by this environment will be. The tropical forests certainly produce much greater variety of niches for animals than do the temperate and arctic environments. However, this theory doesn't explain how the great variety of plant life came into being. The competitive hypothesis is that natural selection in temperate and arctic zones is controlled mainly by the physical environment, whereas biological competition is a more important directive of evolution in the tropics. While organisms in the temperate and arctic zones are more concerned with merely staying alive in the physical environment, animals in the tropics contend with less critical physical conditions. For tropical species, competition and other complex biological factors exert selective pressures to bring about added speciation. A theory of climatic stability, sometimes separated from the former, says that regions with stable climates allow the evolution of finer specializations and adaptations than do areas with erratic climates. It is really just another way of stating the time and competitive hypotheses.

In general, diversity in the tropics is probably due primarily to the great stability and the antiquity of these regions. These and other theories are being tested by ecologists and evolutionists. But it is difficult to test such hypotheses because it is impossible to go back in time, and it is difficult even now to assess the flora and fauna of the tropical rain forest. As I have mentioned before, taxonomists are still discovering new species at a very great rate, which makes comparisons of diversity very difficult.

The living elements of the tropical rain forest can

OPPOSITE:
A rotting stump is all that remains of a proud giant which once shaded this glade in the forest. Light now reaches the understory and stimulates a profusion of growth.

OVERLEAF:
I discovered how this "hairstreak" butterfly managed to move its tails, emulating waving antennas to redirect the attention of a predator: the tails cross at the base and leverage moves them as the wings are rubbed up and down.

be divided into three categories as they participate in the nutrient cycle. These are the producers, consumers, and decomposers. The producers are the plants, all of the plants—the trees, the understory, the herbs, even the epiphytes. These plants take the carbon dioxide from the air and hydrogen and oxygen in the water that they get out of the soil, and turn these elemental substances into sugars. They use the energy of sunlight to carry out the process, which is known as photosynthesis. The sugars are chiefly converted chemically into cellulose. This is the initial stage in the factory of life, and it is absolutely essential for the existence of all other organisms in the forest. Without plants there could be no animals, because animals cannot photosynthesize, cannot produce tissue out of air and water. Other elements are required from the soil for complete plant development.

The consumers follow along behind. They feed on the plants. Like a complex mill, they churn and digest the plant material, and hand over those chemicals which are necessary for life to other consumers amongst themselves. These complexes of consumers constitute the food chain or food web. *Food chain* tends to give the connotation of a single path by which nutrients are transferred from one animal to a second, to a third, and so on in a direct line. *Food web* is probably closer to what really exists, because there isn't a direct line of transfer. A multifold, meshlike transfer takes place from one to another and back and forth among the many components of the system.

Primary consumers eat the leaves directly off the trees and plants of the forest. Secondary consumers, the predators and parasitic animals, feed upon the primary ones. Eventually, each life in the forest comes to an end, every individual of every species eventually dies. This is where the third category, the decomposers, in the nutrient cycle comes in. The nutrients in fallen leaves and twigs—and even in the trunks of giant trees that have been blown over by the wind—are finally handed over to minute organisms, such as termites, wood-boring beetles and caterpillars, and especially bacteria and fungi. These decomposers have the ability to break down cellulose into finer and finer particles, which disintegrate gradually down to their elemental materials. These materials and the degraded tissues of dead animals and their leavings go into the soil. Water in the soil from rain seepage dissolves these substances and elements. They go into solution and reach the depths of the soil where the tree roots can pick them up again. The elements are carried through the vessels of the plants skyward into the leaves, and the whole cycle goes again. So this nutrient cycle is an important requirement of the rain forest and, in fact, of any ecological system.

Zonation, or discontinuous layering or variation, in the rain forest plant types exists both in a vertical and in a horizontal dimension with the controlling factor the same in both cases, the degree of light present. Horizontal zonation is brought about when some factor causes a clearing in the forest. The agent may be man cutting out the forest and letting light in; or, along the edges of a river or stream, it can be water cutting its eternal gravity paths. Whenever a path or clearing is made, light floods in and changes the vegetation. Certain kinds of light-loving plants emerge along the edge of the clearing and, giving way to more shade-tolerant plants, merge finally into the typical, climax rain forest. Two characteristic light-loving plants almost always seen along the edge of clearings are the *Cecropia*, with its jointed trunk and its large palmate leaves, and the common balsawood tree. Many kinds of ferns are also light-loving plants. They are fairly hardy and resist drying. Heliconias are another member of this group of edge-effect plants and a common feature of horizontal zonation. Similarly, looking upward, we find an increase in the number of vines growing along the edge of clearings. Visitors who have traveled up the Amazon or other tropical rivers have

OVERLEAF:
These tiny mushrooms grew like a fairy-tale forest on the decomposing wood at the base of a buttressed stump. The caps are but three-sixteenths of an inch across.

201

frequently described the heavy, dense intermingling of vines along the edge of the river. Such "jungle" growth is not characteristic of the rain forest proper. It is, rather, an edge effect, a part of this horizontal zonation caused by the superabundant growth of plants with access to greater doses of sunlight. Incidentally, *jungle* is a Hindi word applied originally to the dry bush vegetation of the Indian region, quite different from the modern application by the Western world.

In contrast to the horizontal, vertical zonation describes the forest from the forest floor to the uppermost portions of the canopy. One can ascertain different levels or tiers of vegetation. This is a fact which was recognized only when botanists began making a systematic study of the rain forest. Although it may seem that everything from floor to canopy is densely packed with greenery, the rain forest can be broadly divided into five layers. Now, these layers are not perfectly distinct, of course; they have no finite boundaries. They grade together, but they can be recognized in a well-developed rain forest. Starting from the bottom level, we find low-growing herbaceous plants, many soft-leaf flowering plants that are easily crushed by the boots of someone treading through the forest. Often densely green or even reddish in color, they seem to be struggling for every bit

Soft and fleshy, this jelly fungus was found on a dead log by the quebrada one day. Like most of the fungi its name eluded me.

of light, making use of dense amounts of chlorophyll to try and soak up as much light as they possibly can. The next level contains woody shrubs, including large ferns. These are plants which never reach the true proportions of a tree but nevertheless occupy a proper part of the rain forest. Above the zone of woody shrubs are three zones of trees botanically designated *zones*, Zone A, B, and C. Zone C is the lowest, and these are trees of approximately twelve to twenty-five feet in height. In Zone B are trees of thirty-six to seventy-five feet in height, and these form the forest canopy. Zone A trees are the real giants, the real old-timers of the forest, emerging from the canopy and reaching up to one hundred and fifty feet or more. The members of the last two levels are the so-called dominant trees of the rain forest. They often have leaves that are lighter green in color since they have less need for a dense chlorophyll content. Nor do they have the dense green, thick, shiny leaf characteristic of the trees in the lower tiers.

Trees of the lower tiers grow very slowly. They are suppressed in their growth by the dominant trees of the canopy, because light is not able to reach them. It is almost as if they crouch in wait for the time when light is made available by the death of one of the canopy trees. Then they can shoot skyward and take their place as one of the dominant members of the canopy. Few of the seeds of Zone A, the real giants, ever sprout. In the evergreen forests of western Africa, where saplings of Zone A trees are rare, the natives say that these big trees never have children. It is probably because, while all those seeds fall to the floor and germinate, very few of them can survive for lack of light.

Herein lies the central fact of life in the rain forest—competition. In the case of vegetation, two requirements become critical. A plant must have a place to put its roots, and it must have light to photosynthesize. Very often, before it achieves either, it is overshadowed and crowded out.

14. The bath

I'm taking my clothes off right now, trying to get my boots off. I'm going to slip into the stream here, to try a new station from which to reflect on the day. The stream is running well now after that last big rain, the one we had yesterday, and there's a nice pool here, very inviting, about a foot and a half deep. I'm going to slip into it here in a second and settle down and try to give you some account of what happened today.

I'm stark naked now and I'm going to step into the water. Ah, not too cold, I'd say about seventy degrees. Very refreshing, yes, indeed. This was a good idea. I'm just going to lie back here and tell you a little bit about what happened today. Like every day I've been out looking for army ants, and like every day lately I haven't had any luck. I don't want to walk off too far from the

A jungle pool about five miles from the station. The cayman (*Caiman crocodilus*) lives here in company with a breeding pair of tityras in the erect dead log to the left.

station. If I find the army ants too far from the station I can't handle them logistically.

As I have mentioned many times, walking through the forest is very inspiring, and it's hardly possible to go fifty yards along the trail without coming into some kind . . . wow! there are fish in this little pool here. There are about three or four or five, ouch, and there's one kind in particular which seems to like to nibble at my flesh. The last one caused me such a jump that I knocked my tape recorder into the water. (I dried it out, and there's no harm done.) Ouch, damn it! Half a dozen different kinds of fish are in here. They are real beauties. There is a little cyprinodont with a bar running up one side, and half a dozen other grubby-looking fish with a bright black mark near the end of the tail. Then there are some long, slender, wrasselike fishes with a black stripe down the side, which stay near the bottom. There is also a kind of a catfish or sucker on the bottom, which makes it rough when you're taking a bath. And there are the little top minnows swimming near the surface. It certainly is crowded in here.

Many people have talked about the forest, and about its similarity to a church or cathedral, with the spirelike trees, vaulted branches, cloistered corridors, the buttresses, and the echoing sounds. I think I found another analogy today which perhaps hasn't been written about before, and that is that this forest cathedral is complete with stained-glass windows. I ran across a number of leaves today, large leaves that were set in just the right position, among other leaves and the branches of trees, so that the sun was shining through them and casting beautiful reddish-rust hues down through the forest. I stood beneath them and looked up, and thought I was in France, at Chartres.

Another characteristic reminds me of church paraphernalia. In many churches throughout the world, a censer is used to waft incense. This device is roughly

cup-shaped and hangs from a chain. Many birds' nests look just like censers as they hang from tree branches or from the insides of hollow trees. Usually, there's one long thread coming down, which is actually an aerial root from the tree, and the bird very cleverly weaves its nest onto the end of this hanging thread.

Now I see flower petals and even fruits flowing past my legs in the water: little lavender flower petals coming, probably, from quite a distance and drifting past me in the stream. They've fallen out of the tree, which is proof of the·season, proof that the flowering season is past and the fruit are beginning to set and are falling on the forest floor.

I'm trying to decide what similarities there are between seasons in the tropics and those in the temperate zone. Frankly, I don't know whether I'm coming out of

Mouth of the Rio Rincón. Mangroves, principally of the genus *Avicennia*, provide cover for many species of estuarine birds and other animals.

OVERLEAF:
Heliconias and *Cecropia* trees line the margins of a forest stream. The unpolluted waters are home for several species of fish, freshwater crabs, and crayfish.

209

the spring and going into the summer, or coming out of the summer and going into the fall, or coming out of the fall and going into the spring, or what. Certainly, as the rain and the springlike effect comes about, one would expect the flowers to come into bloom, if the scheme here were parallel to that in the temperate regions. Indeed, there are some herbaceous plants beginning to come into flower in response to the rain, but most of the trees have flowered in the dry season, which would correspond to our summer, and now are setting fruit.

There went a basilisk (*Basciliscus basciliscus*) across the water. He hopped upon a limb and I'm watching him now. He seems to be enjoying the water as much as I. He's sitting on a low branch with just the tip of his tail dangling down in the water. He's watching me, and probably has never seen a stranger sight.

Walking along the stream earlier today, I noticed out of the corner of my eye a caterpillar floating in the air alongside me—just floating in the air, dangling without any apparent means of support; flowing along in the breeze about the same velocity as I was walking. I knew, of course, that the caterpillar was hanging from a long strand of silk, although the silk may not have been attached to anything. This phenomenon of small caterpillars and very young spiders dangling in the air from long filaments of thread is called *ballooning*. It is one means of dispersal among certain kinds of animals, those that can produce silk and have lightweight early stages. It is part of their life style to produce a long filament of thread and then to leap off into space and let the air catch up this filament. The longer the filament, the more friction with the air, of course, and the longer distance that the insect can be carried. The creature simply floats off into the breeze and is dispersed, with the filament having the additional property of catching onto vegetation and allowing the insect to find itself a new home more readily. So some of the creatures of my study are trapeze artists and balloonists.

The sunlight flows through dead leaves imparting a golden hue to the air beneath the canopy. These are stained-glass windows of the forest cathedral.

My plan for the day was to work around the stream in the morning until lunchtime, and after lunch to get out into the forest to look for army ants again. One of the things that I wanted to photograph is a log that's lying on the gravel in the stream bed. This log impressed me the first time I came down to it because it looks just exactly like an old man who had been struck down. He fell on his back and is lying in that spot, dead. The log has two branches which look just like two legs, and the trunk is about the right proportion for a torso. The roots of the tree are twisted in such a way that they look like the folded arms of a man lying on his back with his hands extended up toward the sky. Then there's the central taproot which is rounded and short, and gives the impression of the man's head. This is my old man, and I say good morning to him when I go down the stream in the morning. Indeed, I say hello whenever I pass his way and never step on him, for he's the old man of the stream and has, in a way, become a friend of mine.

This dead log lay in the stream bed behind the station and reminded me of a dead man lying on his back.

214

Today, I was reminded by seeing a monarch butterfly that I have some other old friends down here. Some insects and birds, of course, migrate long distances, and there are some here which have migrated from the United States. The monarch butterfly is what brought this to mind today. The monarch is a common species throughout the United States, and is a migratory species. Although they don't migrate as far south as this from the United States; they are here from places like Mexico and they look very much the same. Also, the Baltimore orioles are down here for the winter and so are the chestnut-sided warblers that are common in the eastern United States during the spring and summertime.

Two things are really essential in the way of personal pleasure around here. One is a bath every day, for relaxation and, incidentally, keeping the body clean of fungal spores, bacteria, and so on. The other thing is a siesta. There is something about the midday heat that is extremely oppressive, and to try and work right through the noon hour after working all morning is sheer folly. To have a productive afternoon, it is essential to take a little nap, even for just half an hour.

Around noon today I had an opportunity to make the long trek out toward the other side of the peninsula. An old road goes out that way, and after walking five miles or so, I came upon a gigantic snake, a boa constrictor. He was a big one, about nine feet long, and nice and fat. He was resting coiled up underneath a log, sleeping off the effects of what must have been a very recent meal. With just a little bit of coaxing on my part, he awoke and decided to move out. I walked along beside him. He would stay away from me, and it was very simple to herd him out into a little clearing, a little opening where there was some sun and I was able to get some pictures of him.

The poetry of motion of a snake completely compensates for the fact that these are menacing animals, in general detested by man. But the beauty of movement,

OVERLEAF:
The boa constrictor, a snake with a color pattern that blends its body imperceptibly into the dry leaves of the forest floor.

215

the fluid action of the rippling muscles, and the serpentine flowing of the body of the snake is certainly sufficient for me to consider them beautiful, at least in this one way. The head of a snake to me is ugly, the blunt tail is ugly, and the belly of a snake is ugly. But the back of a snake, its skin and its muscles beneath are beautiful. This snake was a fine specimen because he was so large, so healthy, and so perfect. I could stand behind him and look into the sun and catch the reflection off the scales of his body, which gave off a glowing blue fluorescence. Of course, the skin colors are not bright. The snake is a somber brown, with a mottled pattern to simulate the litter of the forest floor and give him camouflage. The tail has little black rings around it.

It's about five o'clock in the afternoon, and I am still sitting in my bathtub in the stream. The sun is still in the sky, although it has dropped down beyond the trees behind me. It's very nice, cool, and comfortable here. A fellow could get to like this place if it had just a few more of life's pleasures. I will freely admit that.

The goddamned fish are biting me again. But I think they're getting used to me: they seem to know me when I come here, since I come at least once a day now. When I arrive at the pool, there are large fish present, some six and seven inches long, but as soon as I step in, they move away. Only the little ones come up to explore and see what this strange animal is that's invading their privacy.

There is one fish here which is like a marine cleaning wrasse. Now, wrasses are very interesting fish in the sea, and many of them are responsible for keeping parasites cleaned off other fish. They are tolerated by other fish when they come up to them and nibble at their flesh, because what they're doing is taking little arthropod parasites off the bodies of the larger fish. There's a kind of mutual understanding, a symbiotic relationship, which permits these intimacies to take place. In payment for removing the parasites, the wrasse, of course, get a meal. I think about this today and about my bathing in the pool, and about these little wrasses coming up and nibbling at my flesh. Maybe that's what they think they are doing—and, who knows, maybe they are doing me a favor in the same way.

Some people might wonder about bathing in jungle pools. There are, I suppose, some health problems that one could possibly encounter doing this, but such problems as leeches usually develop only in the Old World. Now, there are leeches in the New World, of course, but I've never run into them here in Costa Rica. I've walked around a great deal in wet places in the forest and have not encountered any aquatic leeches. So I bathe without the fear of having them attach themselves to me and of having my blood sucked.

There is another disease which makes a person cautious about putting even a finger in water in Africa, in parts of Brazil, and in parts of the Middle East. It's called Bilharzia or schistosomiasis. This is a disease caused by a trematode worm that lives in the blood system. It gains entrance into the body by means of a stage called a cercaria, which is a microscopic organism that lives in the water. When a person exposes his skin in the water of an infected stream, these organisms burrow into the skin and get into the body, where they metamorphose into adult worms and lodge in the blood vessels. Then they reproduce and go throughout the body, causing serious infection in the spleen, liver, and in other vital organs. The disease is very often fatal. The curious thing about this disease is the complicated life cycle of the parasite. The cercaria develop in a certain kind of snail, which acts as an intermediate host to this organism. When the eggs of the worm get into the digestive tract of the human, they normally get passed into a stream. The eggs hatch into a stage which gets picked up by the snail, and the intermediate stages of the worm go through part of their life cycle in the snail, finally coming out as cercariae. If they are fortunate enough to find a vertebrate host—such as a bathing beauty like myself—they can develop into the troublesome worms. Fortunately, this debilitating disease does not occur here.

Enough of that. But while I'm on the subject of health, I might mention that my bites are clearing up. I think I'm becoming adapted to the substances in the stings and bites of the insects here which have been giving me trouble. I certainly must be being bitten and stung as frequently as ever, but I'm not showing the symptoms nearly as severely. I think it's a natural thing for a person who lives in an area such as this, and who is continually subjected to the stings and bites of insects, to become adapted to them. The body develops a reaction which wards off the poisonous effects.

This gravel gets kind of hard on the tail if you sit on it for a while.

I'm trying to think about a way of conveying the pleasure of the end of the day. There's not a leaf moving on any of the trees. The only movement I see is the little stream here rippling over the rocks. I see the movement of the birds from time to time, but all else is completely still. It makes me feel very strange to be in the midst of all this. It doesn't seem possible that I'm out of doors, for one thing; I always feel as if I'm indoors here. It's because of the height of the trees and the way they grow up around you and make a roof for you. They even protect you from the rain. You can stand in the forest in a heavy downpour for twenty minutes and not get wet—it takes that long for the water to come down.

I feel as if I am indoors almost all the time. It's not the feeling of wide openness that you get from being in the desert or on the great plains. It's a closeness, and this closeness, I think, is what has frightened some people and made them enemies of the forest. On the other hand, the closeness has comforted other people and made them friends of the forest. In a way, you can almost think of

the forest as being like clothing or like your home. It's like a house to you. It's around you, it protects you from the wind and protects you from the rain. It gives you food, it gives you drink, and it gives you pleasure. Of course, there are dangers, but aren't there dangers everywhere? Even in the supposed safety of our civilization and homes in the big cities there's actually more danger, I think, than there is here. If I were to speak in terms of statistics, I probably am safer several times over where I am right now than I would be sitting on a bench waiting for a bus on a downtown street in Los Angeles. I doubt whether many people would agree with that, but I think it is true.

I have my dangers here, I have my enemies, but they are enemies which are enemies only if I make them so, either accidentally or intentionally. The viperous

A katydid nymph with a mottled color pattern that simulates closely the lichens and mosses upon which it habitually feeds and rests.

221

snakes which I've talked about are not going to hurt me unless I do something to frighten them or to injure them. Then they will retaliate. And accidents can occur, of course; but, again, these are accidents which can mostly be avoided, and they're accidents which are precipitated. They aren't like the kinds of accidents that you suffer in automobile traffic. So I do feel safer here. Possibly, part of it is because of my ignorance. I don't know all the things that are going on, I'm sure. Processes must be going on outside of this area which might affect me, which may even lie in store for me, but I can't worry about these. I can't worry about these things, and the forest seems to help me in this. It seems to say, I've been here for millions of years and I'm here, I'm strong, I'm stronger than ever, I'm more beautiful than ever, I'm more diverse than ever, and I know a lot more than you do, and I know that you're going to be all right and we're all going to be here a long time, a long time more.

Pardon me while I finish my bath.

Appendix

Protective function of sound perception
and gregariousness in *Hylesia* larvae
(saturniidae: hemileucinae)*

While in residence at the Tropical Science Center
field station on the Osa Peninsula of Costa Rica (1.8
miles west of Rincón), I was able to make some observations on a colony of *Hylesia* larvae which suggested a
very probable function for their gregarious behavior
and ability to perceive sound.

I first discovered a large aggregation of these
larvae (approximately 330 individuals) in an oval
mass on the trunk of a medium-sized tree, *Trema
micrantha* (Linnaeus), on April 3, 1971. The mass was
located on the north side of the tree about 1 m above
the ground and was about 60 cm in length vertically and

---

* These observations, a result of Dr. Hogue's stay in Costa
Rica, were published originally in the *Journal of the Lepidopterists'
Society* (March 1972).

18 cm in width. I accidentally became aware of the ability of the larvae to perceive sound when I shouted in their direction from a distance of about 10 m. I was amazed to see the entire surface of the mass "jump." Each of the larvae responded to the sound of my voice at the same instant and in the same manner: a violent jerking of the anterior third of the body, so that the head, thorax, and anterior portion of the abdomen were arched upward or sideward.

I tested this reaction numerous times and ways by altering the pitch and loudness of my voice and determined to my satisfaction that the action was due to sound and not to air movement. The larvae reacted only to very sharp and relatively high-pitched sounds of high intensity. Normal conversation did not cause any movement. I further tested the response by playing music (Strauss waltzes) from a tape recorder in the immediate vicinity of the mass (within 1 m) and noted that the larvae responded in the same manner to loud, sharp portions of the music.

I observed the mass for five days. Each day I noted fewer individuals until April 8, at which time there were no longer any present. Several larvae at the beginning had freshly molted, apparently transforming from the penultimate to the final instar. On several occasions during the day, larvae were seen on the ground crawling away from the tree, apparently in search of pupation sites or possibly food. The mass was present on the tree trunk only during the day, migrating at night to another place which was never determined.

This jerking behavior of gregarious lepidopterous larvae in response to sound has been observed and recorded by only a few authors. Minnich (*Journal of Experimental Zoology* 72[1936]:439–453) studied the reaction in the larvae of *Nymphalis antiopa* and records several other species of Lepidoptera which have been noted to behave similarly. None of these accounts, however, offers an explanation for the function of the behavior. Some additional observations which I made on this occasion suggested to me that sound perception coupled with the massing of these larvae served as a protection from parasites.

The larvae were being parasitized by two species, a yellow and black chalcidine wasp and a tachinid fly. The former, on approaching the mass and hovering over it prior to landing and oviposition, elicited the jerking movement. The anterior portions of the caterpillars being thrown dorsally had the effect of warding or fending off the approaching wasps. The denseness of the hairs of the richly branched scoli furnished a barrier to the penetration of the parasites. The larvae in the center of the mass were especially well protected since their flanks were not vulnerable to lateral attacks. The tachinid flies did attempt to approach the larvae from the side by crawling along the bark but were warded off in a similar fashion by lateral jerking. When approaching the mass from above, these flies also elicited the dorsal arching. The high-pitched whining of the wings of the approaching or hovering parasite seemed to be of the correct quality and intensity to elicit the jerking response. The effectiveness of this defensive maneuver is enhanced by the fact that the larvae are densely grouped and heavily clothed with spines and hairs. This behavior would offer much less protection to individual larvae than to larvae en masse.

This protective behavior was not completely successful, however. I observed oviposition by the chalcidine wasps numerous times. Still, the attacking females experienced great difficulty in gaining access to the host's skin through the hair and spine network and violent defensive movements of the mass.

The spines of the scoli are highly urticating to human skin and may also function more effectively in inhibiting attacks from vertebrates by being forced into the skin through this same jerking motion.

A cinematographic record of these observations is on

file with Alan Landsburg Productions, Hollywood, California (Production 1106–02, rolls 157, 158, and 166a). My thanks are extended to that organization for the opportunity to be in the study area and to Julian P. Donahue for assistance in identifying the caterpillars. Unfortunately it was impossible to determine the species of *Hylesia;* several are common at the site.

Bibliography

Allen, P. H. *The rain forests of Golfo Dulce.* Gainesville: University of Florida Press, 1956.

Aubert de la Rue, E.; Bourlière, F.; and Harroy, J.-P. *The tropics.* New York: Alfred A. Knopf, 1957.

Bates, Henry Walter. *The naturalist on the River Amazons.* 1863. Reprint. Berkeley: University of California Press, 1962.

Blake, E. R. *Birds of Mexico: A guide for field identification.* Chicago: University of Chicago Press, 1953.

Dobzhansky, T. "Evolution in the tropics." *American Scientist* 38(1950):209–21.

Eibl-Eibesfeldt, I. and E. "The workers' bodyguard." *Anims' Magazine* 11(1968):16–17.

Faust, E. C.; Beaver, P. C.; and Jung, R. C. *Animal agents and vectors of human disease.* 2d ed. Philadelphia: Lea and Febiger, 1962.

Goodwin, G. G. "Mammals of Costa Rica." *Bulletin of the American Museum of Natural History* 87(1946):271–474.

Gourou, P. *The tropical world: Its social and economic conditions and its future status.* 4th ed. New York: John Wiley and Sons, 1966.

Guenther, K. A. *A naturalist in Brazil: Flora and fauna and the people of Brazil.* Translated by Bernard Miall. London: George Allen & Unwin, Ltd., 1931.

von Hagen, V. W., ed. *The green world of the naturalists: A treasury of five centuries of natural history in South America.* New York: Greenberg, 1948.

Hinton, H. E. "Myrmecophilous Lycaenidae and other Lipidoptera—A summary." *Transactions of the South London Entomological and Natural History Society* 1949–50:111–75.

Holdridge, L. R. "The tropics: A misunderstood ecosystem." *Bulletin of the Association for Tropical Biology* 5(1965):21–50.

Holdridge, L. R., et al. *Forest environments in tropical life zones: A pilot study.* Oxford: Pergamon Press, 1971.

Jamieson, B. G. M., and Reynolds, J. F. *Tropical plant types.* Oxford: Pergamon Press, 1967.

Janzen, D. H. "Co-evolution of mutualism between ants and acacias in Central America." *Evolution* 20(1966):249–75.

———. "Allelopathy by myrmecophytes: The ant *Azteca* as an allelopathic agent of *Cecropia.*" *Ecology* 50(1969):147–53.

———. "Synchronization of sexual reproduction of trees within the dry season in Central America." *Evolution* 21(1967):620–27.

Janzen, D. H., and Schoener, T. W. "Differences in insect abundance and diversity between wetter and drier sites during a tropical dry season." *Ecology* 49(1968):96–109.

Johnson, R. A. "The behavior of birds attending army ant raids on Barro Colorado Island, Panama Canal Zone." *Proceedings of the Linnaean Society of New York* 63–65(1951–1953):41–70.

Kirkpatrick, T. W. *Insect life in the tropics.* London: Longmans, 1957.

Knight, D. H. *A field guide to the trees of Barro Colorado Island, Panama Canal Zone.* University of Wyoming and Smithsonian Tropical Research Institute, 1970.

Land, H. C. *Birds of Guatemala.* Wynewood, Pa.: Livingston Pub. Co., 1970.

Lloyd, J. E. "Aggressive mimicry in *Photuris:* firefly femmes fatales." *Science* 149(1965):653–54.

———. "Bioluminescent communication in insects." *Annual Revue of Entomology* 16(1971):97–122.

Malicky, H. "New aspects on the association between lycaenid larvae (Lycaenidae) and ants (Formicidae, Hymenoptera)." *Journal of the Lepidopterists' Society* 24(1970):190–202.

Martin, M. M. "The biochemical basis of the fungus–attine ant symbiosis." *Science* 169(1970):16–20.

Matthews, R. W. "Nesting biology of the social wasp *Microstigmus comes* (Hymenoptera: Sphecidae, Pemphredoninae)." *Psyche* 75(1967):23–45.

Moser, J. C. "Trails of the leafcutters." *Natural History* 76(1967):33–35.

Organization for Tropical Studies. Miscellaneous student reports and study guides. Mimeographed. San José, Costa Rica, 1962–1970.

Pianka, E. R. "Latitudinal gradience in species diversity: A review of concepts." *American Naturalist* 100(1966):33–43.

van der Pijl, L., and Dodson, C. H. *Orchid flowers: Their pollination and evolution*. Coral Gables: University of Miami Press, 1966.

Rau, P. *The jungle bees and wasps of Barro Colorado Island (with notes on other insects)*. St. Louis: privately published, 1933.

Rettenmeyer, C. W. "Observations on the biology and taxonomy of flies found over swarm raids of army ants (Diptera: Tachinidae, Conopidae)." *University of Kansas Science Bulletin* 42(1961): 993–1066.

————. "Behavioral studies of army ants." *University of Kansas Science Bulletin* 44(1963):281–465.

Richards, P. W. *The tropical rain forests: An ecological study*. Cambridge: Cambridge University Press, 1964.

Ross, G. N. "Life-history studies on Mexican butterflies. IV. The ecology and ethology of *Anatole rossi*, a myrmecophilous metalmark (Lepidoptera: Riodinidae)." *Annals of the Entomological Society of America* 59(1966):985–1004.

de Schauensee, R. M. *The birds of Colombia and adjacent areas of South and Central America*. Norberth, Pa.: Livingston Pub. Co., 1964.

Schneirla, T. C. *Army ants: A study in social organization*. Edited by N. Topof. San Francisco: Freeman & Co., 1971.

Shuttleworth, F. S.; Zim, H. S.; and Dillon, G. W. *Orchids*. New York: Golden Press, 1970.

Silverberg, R. *The world of the rain forest*. New York: Meredith Press, 1967.

Slud, P. "The birds of Costa Rica, distribution and ecology." *Bulletin of the American Museum of Natural History* 128(1964): 1–430.

Spurr, S. H. *Forest ecology*. New York: Roth Press, 1964.

Sudd, J. H. *An introduction to the behavior of ants*. New York: St. Martin's Press, 1967.

Torgerson, R. L., and Akre, R. D. "Interspecific responses to trail and alarm pheromones by New World army ants." *Journal of the Kansas Entomological Society* 43(1970):395–404.

Weber, N. A. "Fungus growing ants." *Science* 153(1966):587–604.

Wheeler, W. M. *Ants: Their structure, development and behavior*. New York: Columbia University Press, 1913.

————. "Studies of neotropical ant plants and their ants." *Bulletin of the Museum of Comparative Zoology* 90(1942):1–262.

Index

232

PHOTO CREDITS

The photos on the following pages were taken by Julian P. Donahue: xviii, 3, 12, 14–15, 16, 18, 32, 36–37, 68 (left), 84, 100 (bottom), 114–15, 118, 147, 151, 152, 153 (top), 154, 168, 172–73, 175, 178, 192–93, 195, 221. The remaining photos were taken by the author.

Beaulieu camera used exclusively in the New Explorers expeditions.